URBAN RE-INDUSTRIALIZATION

Before you start to read this book, take this moment to think about making a donation to punctum books, an independent non-profit press

@ https://punctumbooks.com/support

If you're reading the e-book, you can click on the image below to go directly to our donations site. Any amount, no matter the size, is appreciated and will help us to keep our ship of fools afloat. Contributions from dedicated readers will also help us to keep our commons open and to cultivate new work that can't find a welcoming port elsewhere. Our adventure is not possible without your support.
Vive la open-access.

Fig. 1. Hieronymus Bosch, *Ship of Fools* (1490–1500)

First published in 2017 by punctum books, Earth, Milky Way.
https://punctumbooks.com

ISBN-13: 978-1-947447-02-8 (print)
ISBN-13: 978-1-947447-03-5 (ePDF)

LCCN: 2017945435
Library of Congress Cataloging Data is available from the Library of Congress

Copy-editing: Cheryl Jaworski
Interior design: Vincent W.J. van Gerven Oei
Cover design: Architectural drawing by Dan Green

HIC SVNT MONSTRA

# URBAN
## RE-INDUSTRIALIZATION

Krzysztof Nawratek, editor

Ⓟ

# Contents

PART 3: HOW SHOULD WE DO IT?

# Acknowledgments

This book has emerged as a result of two mini-conferences I organised at the Plymouth University: 'Re-Industrialisation and Progressive Urbanism' in 2013 and 'Industrious Ecologies: Reclaiming the Subjectivity of the City' in 2014. The main inspiration for these events (and subsequently the book) came from the work of the Master of Architecture programme I was leading from 2012 to 2015, and from discussions with professor Michelle Adams from Dalhousie University, who also gave me the idea for the structure of this book. I am also grateful to Eileen A. Joy who enthusiastically reacted to the book proposal and to Vincent W.J. van Gerven Oei for his work as an editor.

Introduction

# Urban Re-Industrialization As a Political Project

*Krzysztof Nawratek*

Urban re-industrialization could be seen as a method of in-creasing business effectiveness in the context of a politically stimulated 'green economy'; it could also be seen as a nostalgic mutation of a creative-class concept, focused on 3D printing, 'boutique manufacturing' and crafts. These two notions place urban re-industrialization within the context of the current neoliberal economic regime and urban development based on property and land speculation. Could urban re-industrializa-tion be a more radical idea? Could urban re-industrialization be imagined as a progressive socio-political and economic project, aimed at creating an inclusive and democratic society based on cooperation and a symbiosis that goes way beyond the current model of a neoliberal city?

In January 2012, against the backdrop of the financial crisis that began in 2008, Krzysztof Nawratek (leader of the Master of Architecture program at Plymouth University) published a text in opposition to the fantasy of a 'cappuccino city' arguing that the post-industrial city is a fiction, and that it should be replaced by 'Industrial City 2.0'.

The Master of Architecture program at Plymouth University has been working on a vision of such a city for the last few years. The idea of urban re-industrialization appeared, in some senses organically, when in 2009 they were invited to Riga, to look at the Andrejsala peninsula, which is an area that Rem Koolhaas and his company OMA (Office for Metropolitan Architecture) prepared a master plan for. The plan envisaged the construction of luxury apartments for thirty thousand inhabitants (Riga during this time had been losing 10,000 residents per year), supplemented by a modern art museum. However, the financial crisis of 2008 made this plan irrelevant. This was a typical 'cappuccino city' project, targeting the urban middle classes, and expecting them to magically appear in a post-socialist city. This type of thinking doesn't bother to ask questions about where the middle classes (or indeed their money) are coming from; it just assumes that they are 'somewhere out there', and that they will come and spend their money and spare time indulging in expensive restaurants and a range of cultural activities.

Industrial City 2.0 is an attempt to see a post-socialist and post-industrial city from another perspective, a kind of negative of the modernist industrial city. If, for logistical reasons and because of a concern for the health of residents, modernism tried to separate different functions from each other (mainly industry from residential areas), the Industrial City 2.0 must be based on the ideas of coexistence, proximity and synergy. A good example of this is shown in a design by Jonathan Pickford, a former Master of Architecture student, for Riga. He proposed the creation of a state-funded 'industrial think-tank' connected with a small factory and a technical school that focused on timber processing as catalysts for further development. On the one hand the project envisaged a use of timber, the only natural resource Latvia possesses, and on the other tied this in with the local tradition of timber buildings and modern, timber-based industrial design, mainly developed in nearby Scandinavia. This concept was then developed in the coming years in Gdańsk, Zielona Góra, Warsaw and Cieszyn, and was based on a similar search for synergies between different urban processes and the idea of an inclusive city, a city for all its residents. These projects were located in a context of a post-socialist and neo-liberal city and were based on invitations from local institutions or organizations. But so far none of them has been developed any further.

Are they all just theoretical exercises? Is urban re-industrialization a valid concept at all?

In this book Jeffrey T. Kruth's chapter presents an example of the 'Health-Tech Corridor', which was developed in Cleveland, Ohio, proving that if cities are shrinking and neoliberalism creates bankrupt companies and wastelands, progressive re-industrialization could be a way towards an alternative, effective economic model. This does not happen by itself, of course: a political will is required to cut off (at least for a while) a fragment of the economy that supports the neoliberal logic of immediate profit at any cost. At the heart of the 'Health-Tech Corridor' is the Cleveland Clinic, which, like the university and several other key institutions, is a not-for-profit organization, which allows considerable tax relief. Kruth discusses the importance of mechanisms to avoid land speculation and to base the economy on income and business taxation. Cleveland is not the only example of a successful industrial cluster associated with a clinic and a university. Evergreen Cooperative is a cooperative enterprise, and owner of, amongst others, the Green City Grower, which is one of the largest hydroponic farms in the United States and plays a significant role in a development of the city. It is interesting that Evergreen is by no means a grassroots mobilization model but is based on close cooperation with the most important local institutions and enterprises.

The Cleveland example is important because it shows two key aspects of contemporary, progressive re-industrialization: firstly, that re-industrialization becomes possible where the city is shrinking and neoliberalism is unable to sustain itself on land and property speculation (for it also proves that neoliberalism is *not* the most effective economic regime), and secondly, that contemporary re-industrialization should be closely linked with a progressive, social economy, one that tries to take into account the social and environmental costs of production. Such an economy requires a rebuilding of the social context in which it operates because it has to earn acceptance and support from the local community, and it also has to satisfy the material and ethical needs of that community. Similar issues are discussed in the chapter by Karl Baker, which examines enterprises that allow the general public to 'look inside', and somehow to control the working conditions of employees and the environmental standards. The 'Transparent factory' could also put industrial production, as a kind of a spectacle, at the center of the social and cultural life of the city.

Of course, urban re-industrialization does not have to be a progressive, emancipatory and inclusive political project. As Kate Royston shows in her chapter, it could still be adjusted by capitalist logic to increase productivity and diminish waste. Conditions which may allow for a radical paradigm shift are analyzed by Michael Edwards and Myfawny Taylor but also by Tatjana Schneider. In a similar way, Malcolm Miles connects re-industrialization with solidarity built on common activities. Krzysztof Nawratek uses Ernst Junger's idea of 'total mobilization' to argue for urban re-industrialization as a new universalism. Alison Hulme examines the various phenomena of Chinese industrial urbanization, existing parallel to the mainstream neoliberal strand, paying attention primarily to those that grew from the bottom up, mobilizing different parts of Chinese society and Chinese culture in a multidimensional synergy. China is also the focus in the chapter by Kevin Lo and Mark Wang, who analyze the impact of the regulation of $CO_2$ emissions on the economy of China, arguing that although in the short term adjustments reduce the possibility of the development of Chinese industry, in the long term regulations stimulate innovation and the development of high-tech industry. John R. Bryson, Jennifer Clark and Rachel Mulhall consider the consequences of decentralized production mainly based on 3D printing for future cities and homes, and Doreen Jakob goes further to consider the consequences of decentralized capitalism, pointing to the promises and weaknesses of crowd- sourcing projects. Jakob observes the non-democratic nature of these types of urbanization. Karol Kurnicki introduces a 'loss', as a third aspect, in addition to production and consumption, of the discussion of re-industrialisation. Loss is what opens up the production to a change, to innovation, to the unknown. Jonathan Vickery tracks the progressive elements supporting cultural and material production in the documents of the European Union.

The presented texts are attempting to create a framework for a better, more just and more democratic world, linking social progress closely to technological progress and industry. Urban re-industrialization could and should become an integral part of the chain of knowledge production and for fulfilling human needs. These texts argue that social progress must go hand in hand with technological progress and that urban re-industrialization is a key component of both.

Chapter 1

# Re-Industrialization as Progressive Urbanism
## Why and How?

*Michael Edwards and Myfanwy Taylor*

## Introduction

This book, like the conference which led to it, is part of an essential and expanding discussion which criticizes the fundamental structure of contemporary economy and society and examines the scope for long-term alternatives and worthwhile immediate interventions, demands and experiments.[1] The context is partly a historical one. Over thousands of years, but especially since the emergence of capitalism a few centuries ago, we have moved away from forms of society where needs were almost always met locally, from local resources and with rather little division of labor or division of time between 'production', 'distribution', 'consumption', caring, nurturing, playing and all the other things people do to the elaborate divisions of labor outlined below. Although anthropologists, archaeologists and historians continue to expose and refine our understanding of the

---

1  There are intersections with the de-growth movements, research and practice in social innovations, many green movements, and Occupy and other emerging urban social movements. Some of these are discussed later in the chapter, while others are linked from the bibliography.

actual course of events, it is very useful to think in terms of the progressive shifts from a stylized subsistence society in which exchange was highly localized, long-distance trade limited to rare materials (gold, spices) and products of extreme skill or art (scythes, ornaments, fine utensils, weapons).[2] We can think of the settlements and architectural expressions of such societies as relatively un-differentiated buildings, with specialized building types emerging alongside specialization in manufacture (forges, grain mills, boatyards), in the reproduction of population, collective services and social control (schools, hospitals, churches and mosques, prisons) and the infrastructure required (ports, canals, railways, water supply systems), all of which are profoundly influential in the formation of our cities. The counterpart to that is evolution of non-residential built forms has been the dwelling, robbed of most of its earlier functions and now reduced — for most of us — to a box for sleeping, eating, child-raising and private, individualized consumption. Many of the physical structures we now take for granted are the distinct products of exploitative systems of supervision and control of 'work' — the factory, the office building — systems which may now, for some, become obsolete through virtual control of distributed work and through casualized self-employment in which we manage our own exploitation.[3] Two other features of modern capitalism are relevant to this issue of 're-industrialization': the growth of globalization, especially of trade and money-flows, and the dual role of buildings and land as having both use value and asset value. The explosive growth of international trade has tended to integrate previously-localized economies and at the

2   Paul. Seabright, *The Company of Strangers* (Princeton: Princeton University Press, 2004) and David. Graeber, *Debt: The First 5000 Years* (Brooklyn: Melville House, 2011), are two outstanding long views.

3   Richard. Sennett, *The Corrosion of Character: The Personal Consequences of Work in the New Capitalism* (New York: W.W. Norton, 1998); Madeleine Bunting, *Willing Slaves: How the Overwork Culture Is Ruling Our Lives* (London: Harper Collins, 2011).

same time transform them.[4] Thus in recent decades the growing mass of profits accumulating in the world has tended disproportionately to be invested in manufacturing production, where labor is cheap and authoritarian regimes can keep it so; elsewhere investment has focussed on extraction of hydrocarbons, metals and other minerals; and elsewhere again (strongly here in the UK) a major focus of investment has been in land and property, driving up housing and premises values and costs as investors seek rents. This is profoundly important for settlements and buildings which increasingly are produced and managed as 'assets' to satisfy investment markets, rather than simply as what is useful or desired by citizens. All of this is both a consequence and an engine of globalization. The availability of cheap container shipping and extremely cheap manufactured goods, mainly from Asia, has made it possible for wages in the global north to remain static or to decline in real terms, while workers have been paying more for fuel and rent and profits grow. Meanwhile, money capital has been increasingly free to move to exploit these changing patterns of extraction of social surplus and support the credit-fueled maintenance of consumption. Many of these mechanisms are lucidly unpacked in the work of the geographer David Harvey and are linked with food and energy crises (and their related land grabs) by the economist Alain Lipietz.[5] These social processes are large-scale, spanning the geography of the whole world and penetrating the most remote and previously autonomous regions. Meanwhile, marketized relations penetrate into spheres of life previously outside the commodity economy — child and elderly care, recreation and sport, education — replacing reciprocity and free, collective provision and ratcheting up the charges for utilities and social housing.

---

4   Andrew Glyn, *Capitalism Unleashed: Finance, Globalization, and Welfare* (Oxford: Oxford University Press, 2006).

5   David Harvey, *The Enigma of Capital and the Crises of Capitalism* (London: Profile, 2010); Alain Lipietz, 'Fears and Hopes: The Crisis of the Liberal-Productivist Model and Its Green Alternative', *Capital & Class* 37, no. 1 (2013): 127–41.

## What might provoke change?

A variety of circumstances may start to reverse some of these trends, prompting what the organizers of this conference have termed 're-industrialization'. Reduction in world trade could come from (a) a general contraction of global activity in the crisis; (b) rising relative wages and production costs in China and other countries, reducing their competitive advantage; (c) increases in the cost of freight transport through rising oil prices or through taxation, or even enforcement aimed at ending marine/aviation pollution; or (d) protectionist measures by national or EU governments. Some of these tendencies are already visible on a small scale and it's worth reflecting on what could cause each to accelerate. These forces in combination could impel economies like the UK's towards greater self-sufficiency in raw materials, in manufacturing (and even in certain services, like tourism). Most of those factors don't apply at a regional scale but affect whole nations. Rising transport costs, however, would be an important factor in redistributing activity within the country, fostering more localized production and compressing supply chains, which means there are more local materials in construction, local brewing again and fewer Cornish potatoes going to be scrubbed in Lincolnshire and then sent to shops in Bristol. It's worth taking great care with words in this discussion. In particular, the term 'post-industrial society' is to be avoided, because our society is just as dependent as it ever was on 'industry'. Much of the production we depend on nowadays takes place abroad, so that fewer of us do factory jobs in Europe and many people under about thirty may never have entered a factory. But whether we use 'industry' in the sense of 'hard work' or loosely, as an approximation for manufacturing, we are utterly dependent on it. Perhaps individual cities which have experienced dramatic deindustrialization can more accurately be called 'post-industrial cities', but it is important to recognize that even in a city such as London there remain significant portions of land currently labelled for industrial use and many workers still deal with physical goods. Groups such as Just Space and the London Thames Gateway Forum are currently campaigning to prevent such spaces from being converted for office use or housing use. We therefore need to be careful that 're-industrialization' doesn't blind us to the industry that already exists, even in primarily service economies.

## Re-industrialization as progressive urbanism?

This takes us to the issue of why *re-industrialization* might be something we want to propose or encourage. There are multiple answers to this question, and we are not all coming from the same positions. In one corner, there are those who strongly reject today's rampant capitalism — or capitalism of any kind. Another strand is the critique of the conceptualization of 'the economy' as just the money-traded part of social life, valuing output on a market basis and devaluing much of society's most precious activities and skills. A third strand is the imperative to take full account of environmental impacts in measuring and valuing activity, and to reconfigure activity to stop or reverse environmental damage. A fourth strand will be the multiple demands to re-humanize work,[6] reduce our alienation from what we 'produce' and 'consume', transform social relations in work groups and retain the full value of people's labor under their individual, collective and/or local control.[7] These are, of course not rival or competing arguments — they intersect and are mutually reinforcing. This conference has specifically asked us to consider re-industrialization as a route to a more progressive urbanism. This takes us directly to the issue of the *nature* of urban growth which a re-industrialization strategy might generate, and whether this might be considered to be more or less progressive than present approaches, or indeed other alternative strategies. Presently, urban growth strategies tend to be in-

---

6   Richard Sennett, *The Craftsman* (New Haven: Yale University Press, 2008).

7   Jamie Gough, 'Neoliberalism and Socialisation in the Contemporary City: Opposites, Complements and Instabilities', *Antipode* 34, no. 3 (2002): 405–26.

formed by powerful narratives that position a small proportion of the activities that go on in cities as productive and generative. We are all familiar with *global* cities, *creative* cities, *high-tech* cities, etc. As Doreen Massey's work on London[8] has shown, these perspectives imply that the interests of all lie in the performance of these sub-sectors of cities' economies. In fact, as we know, urban growth strategies that privilege high-skilled and high-income activities over all others tend to increase inequality, at the same time as they produce riches for the few. Researchers studying cities in the global South know this only too well,[9] recognizing that the means by which the poor make cities work are at risk of being neglected or even destroyed through the application of such narrowly-framed strategies. In this context, perhaps the most powerful contribution the notion of 're-industrialization' can make is to unsettle these dominant narratives by positioning a very different set of activities in the driving seat of future urban development. Even in a so-called 'global city' such as London, industrial activities play an essential role in making the urban economy work. Simple industrial surveying by the London Thames Gateway Forum has exposed clusters of specialist lift manufacture and repair companies, for example, which are able to respond rapidly and competently to lift breakdowns in London's tubes and offices, as well as aggregate yards, whose central riverside location meant that aggregates could be transported by river and rail rather than road, minimizing air pollution. Re-Industrialization prompts us to look again at these neglected industrial activities and to ask how they might be connected to other urban activities. This is also important in light of the evidence that firms benefit from the co-presence of same-sector and different-sector firms,[10] and that it is the collective coordination of urban activities amongst firms and

---

8  Doreen Massey, *World City* (Cambridge: Polity Press, 2007).

9  Jennifer Robinson, *Ordinary Cities: Between Modernity and Development* (Oxford: Routledge, 2006).

10  Gilles Duranton and Diego Puga, 'Nursery Cities: Urban Diversity, Process Innovation, and the Life-Cycle of Products', *American Economic Review* 91, no. 5 (2001): 1454–77.

other economic actors that creates agglomeration economies.[11] If we are interested in progressive urbanism, however, we perhaps ought to go further than 're-industrialization'. Some of the other contributors to this book and the associated conference are hopeful about a humanizing re-industrialization, in which engaged work as a maker, perhaps in the 21st-century industry of mass customization, transforms our relations of production. Others are hopeful about the potential of re-industrialization to drive the ecological changes we are concerned to see. What we are missing, perhaps, is a specifically feminist perspective, alert to the ways in which whole aspects of life have been ignored by mainstream approaches to cities and the economy. Feminist geographers have showed how cities rely on the unpaid work of women and men in connecting the realms of work and life,[12] while feminist economists have been at pains to demonstrate the value of unpaid work in conventional economic terms.[13] What this work has shown us is that unless and until we re-think 'the economy', our efforts to achieve more progressive urbanisms will face some serious limitations.[14] Re-Industrialization has much going for it as a starting point for thinking about progressive urbanism. It offers the potential to re-connect with meaningful and humanizing work in cities, and to begin to adapt the ways our cities work to avert ecological crisis. It moves in direct opposition to many of the recent developments towards globalization and modern capitalism, as well as against the dominant

11 Allen Scott and Michael Storper, 'Regions, Globalization, Development', *Regional Studies* 37, no. 6–7 (2003): 579–93.

12 Linda McDowell et al., 'The Contradictions and Intersections of Class and Gender in a Global City: Placing Working Women's Lives on the Research Agenda', *Environment and Planning A* 37 (2005): 441–61; Helen Jarvis, 'Moving to London Time: Household Co-ordination and the Infrastructure of Daily Life', *Time & Society* 14 (2005): 133.

13 Jenny Cameron and Julie Katherine Gibson-Graham, 'Feminising the Economy: Metaphors, Strategies, Politics', *Gender, Place & Culture* 10, no. 2 (2003): 145–57.

14 Julie Katherine Gibson-Graham, *The End of Capitalism (As We Knew It): A Feminist Critique of Political Economy* (Minneapolis: University of Minnesota Press, 2006), first published in 1996 by Blackwell.

narratives of how urban economies work and the narrow city strategies they inform. As such, it powerfully opens up the more important — and yet neglected — question of who or what cities and their economies are for.[15] At the heart of a progressive urbanism would be a concern for life as well as work and for the ways in which they together make our urban lives possible.

---

15  Massey, *World City.*

Chapter 2

# Mechanisms of Loss

*Karol Kurnicki*

## Introduction

Even without recalling the generalizing notion of 'human nature', it is not excessive to suggest that human activity is creation.
The delimitation in human life between work, learning, leisure
or play is useful in as much as it allows for the analysis of different segments of social reality. However, in spite of its conveni-
ence, this delimitation is artificial and problematic because it
hides relations which are based on the production of new things
on the level of everyday practices. These relations engage various resources and link different levels of social life which always
resist categorization and analytical simplification. Everything
is — or can be — production. Everything is a social product.[1]

The ideologies of the post-industrial city,[2] which are widely
accepted in developed countries, induce a concentration on the
maintenance of the privileges of a comfortable life that are far
away from the real conditions of its reproduction. This situation
is not only unaltered, but is reinforced by the demands imposed
on people and the things that people demand of themselves: being creative at work, having fun, creating a pleasant personal

1   Henri Lefebvre, *Dialectical Materialism,* trans. J. Sturrock (Minneapolis:
    University of Minnesota Press, 2009), 102–20.
2   See, for example, Richard Florida, *Cities and the Creative Class* (New York:
    Routledge, 2005); Charles Landry, *The Creative City: A Toolkit for Urban
    Innovators* (London: Comedia, 2008).

image for others (as consumers), undertaking constant efforts to prove oneself valuable for existing modes of production, etc. In this context, it is often seen as more important to make a good choice of colors on the custom-made Nike trainers than to be aware of the social and economic networks that made their existence possible. Production and creation go hand-in hand with consumer individualism.

## Problems with re-industrialization

In the urban context of developed regions, the question of re-industrialization is entangled with two major issues. First are the overproduction of goods and the domination of consumerism, which can basically be seen as two sides of the same coin. The second issue regards an overtone of international competition and rivalry which is difficult to sustain in the globalized world.

Re-industrialization, as with any other economic process, raises questions about its entanglement with social relations. It is particularly so if we accept that re-industrialization is not only a way out of the recent economic crisis or about simply relocating factories, but is primarily a social activity, and that the restoration of industrial production is important for society. For a consumer, it is often irrelevant whether the product he or she purchases was made fifteen, fifty or five thousand kilometers away, especially if the price stays the same. To pose the question in a different way: is the geographical location of industry pertinent in a situation when it serves as a means to maintaining existing relations, defending old welfare states, reproducing power structures or supporting society as a consumers' assembly?

It seems that the problem here is again that of external context, i.e. a set of criteria which can be used to evaluate social development or to choose a more or less pro-social political economy. Despite the impossibility of returning to the modernist ideals of progress, which not so long ago supported beliefs in slogans such as the one adopted by German carmaker Audi ('*Vorsprung durch Technik*', meaning 'Advancement through technology'), strong ideas should not be abandoned. Critique of contemporary modes of production, with its center–periphery divide or its impossibility of negative judgement of seemingly free consumerism (manifest in modern-day proverbs such as 'the customer is always right' and 'the market is free'), is problematic. It is so not for the reason that it takes an extraneous position full of dignified superiority. It is rather because of its inability to create its own system of convincing ideas and solutions, which would form a positive, adequate and viable proposition. The fact that tools of social and political critique are widely known and available, does not translate to their usage. Luc Boltanski argues that there is a need to create an analytical framework which would integrate what he calls an 'overarching programme' with a 'pragmatic programme'.[3] The former provides an external and general picture of social order, including something which can be called 'commensurability' (or 'principles of equivalence', in Boltanski's terminology). The latter turns its attention to the competences of actors and their actions as well as their own justifications for those actions.

Re-industrialization could be an ideology which has more widespread social meaning and influence, providing that it is defined as a tool for as precise as possible, and at the same time (auto-)reflexive, social operations. What we learned from historical social processes of de-industrialization was that the transformation of social models and breaks with development paths over a hundred years old is possible in a very short time.[4] It means that new reconfigurations are possible, even more so since some elements of this possibility are already available. However, it should imply the rejection of a currently functioning, clear-cut division between production and consumption, producer and consumer. Instead of asking what and where something can be

---

3   Luc Boltanski, *On Critique: Sociology of Emancipation,* trans. G. Elliott (Cambridge: Polity Press, 2011), 48.

4   Such was the nature of neoliberal restructuring; see Neil Brenner and Nik Theodore, 'Cities and the Geographies of "Actually Existing Neoliberalism"', in *Spaces of Neoliberalism: Urban Restructuring in North America and Western Europe,* eds. Neil Brenner and Nik Theodore, 2–32 (Oxford: Blackwell Publishing, 2002).

produced, we should be asking for what and for whom is a given thing valuable? Additionally, we should ask how to make conversion between production and consumption at the same time smoother and more complicated? To put it differently, the issue here is about procedures linking economic transformation and material practices with conditions of existence on the level of individual actions and justifications. Moreover, in the wider social context it should be possible to relate the above- mentioned elements with ideas such as 'for the common good' or of 'right to the city', as defined by Lefebvre.[5] Accordingly, and for the same reasons, referring to the ideals of universal and everyday social emancipation would be appropriate. Secondly, and only begrudgingly mentioned, the reason for re-industrialization is the economic success of countries and cities outside of Europe and North America, with simultaneous worsening of the situation in these two regions of the world, epitomized by post-Fordism[6] and the resultant reshuffling of welfare state systems.[7] For some time now, it seems that developed countries are losing the ability to create their own history, not to mention to decide about the fate of the world. If we believe Wallerstein, it has to do with the general, and possibly long-lasting, crisis of the modern world-system.[8] Re-industrialization could be used as one of means of escaping this crisis. The question is, can it be used only in a reactionary way? It does not seem to be a big problem to re-establish industry as a pillar of developed countries, especially as it is still an important element of their economies and continues to form a significant share of their GDPs.[9] However, for better or for worse, it would not mean returning to the era of bright and

5   Henri Lefebvre, 'Right to the City', in *Writings on Cities*, trans. E. Kofman and E. Lebas, 147–59 (Oxford: Blackwell, 2000).

6   Krishan Kumar, *From Post-Industrial to Post-Modern Society: New Theories of the Contemporary World*, 2nd edn. (Malden: Blackwell Publishing, 2005).

7   Gøsta Esping-Andersen, *Social Foundations of Postindustrial Economies* (Oxford: Oxford University Press, 2003).

8   Immanuel Wallerstein, *World-Systems Analysis: An Introduction* (Durham: Duke University Press, 2006).

9   World Bank, http://data.worldbank.org/indicator/NV.IND.TOTL.ZS.

brave modernization. Thus, the more important issue is a creation of mechanisms of re-industrialization. These mechanisms
could operate to facilitate and strengthen social relations, which
would in turn enable the development of alternatives to the current and existing mode of 'creative destruction', especially that
it currently becomes less and less creative. Another issue is that
the term 're-industrialization' itself implies a certain geographical perspective. While Western countries were experiencing a
dismantling of industry, many peripheral regions have started
to industrialize and grow economically. In fact, (re-)industriali-
zation is constantly happening. Unfortunately, as it is controlled
from London or New York and based on outdated Western patterns, it usually produces or reproduces conditions which were
shared by European or American workers in the past.[10]

## Dialectics of loss/surplus

The dialectical relation mentioned above between producer and
consumer is at once the strength, and also the biggest problem,
of existing modes of production. Paradoxically, it is something
that, in a new form and within a different context, should be
retained for use in re-industrialization processes. Every per-
son and social institution can be perceived as both a creative
producer of objects and other goods, and a consumer. The relation here is analogical between a human and space. Although
we cannot determine the exact properties of this relation, it
does not mean that the reciprocal influence is not real. The key
problem of such a relation is that it does not enable change. Of
course, we can accept that there is a margin of free choice. We
can use one space but not another, go to work for a seemingly
better company or buy a shampoo with conditioner or without.
The fact remains that it is a closed system and that those free
choices and the current social conditions are not transformed
but reproduced. As observed by Lefebvre, "the opposition be-

---

10  Saskia Sassen, *Cities in a World Economy*, 3rd ed. (Thousand Oaks: Pine
Forge Press, 2006).

tween production and consumption [...] cannot completely mask the dialectical conflict suggested by the term 'productive consumption'".[11] Is there really nothing else to do but take the external position of critique and bring to light contradictions caused by the aforementioned opposition? There might be another way which is related both to breaching the dialectics of production and consumption and to the possibility of a critique grounded in real, everyday human actions.

Every instance of production and consumption comprise a loss. It might be a by-product, waste, trash, unused energy, an empty lot or even the opening of new possibilities which cannot be taken at the given moment. A loss can be a third element, supplementing production and consumption. In other words, a loss can be a surplus, an excess, a resource for further use. Moreover, in relation to production and consumption it can function as a correcting element, disrupting a simple binary opposition. Importantly, this three-way relation is not logical but dialectical, although by its character it is different from traditional linear dialectics, which dictate that the end of a workday means leisure and consumption, after which there is another day of work.

Using the most evident example of rubbish as a symbol of loss, we can notice how in some situations it is considered problematic, while in others it becomes a resource which enables the constitution of a third important element and a complication of the binary production-consumption duo. In the first instance, the loss resulting from production or consumption is managed by means which negate its value. The only solution for loss is then either its complete exclusion from circulation or — and this is a more contemporary capitalist (and ecological) way — its reintroduction to the system as a part of production or consumption. In the meantime, the qualitative difference of loss is gone. In many countries, rubbish is a property of those who create it until it is collected from the street or a backyard by (often private) cleaning services. Paying for rubbish collection means

---

11 Henri Lefebvre, *The Production of Space*, trans. D. Nicholson Smith (Oxford: Blackwell, 2010), 354.

that, even within the green and seemingly circular politics of recycling, waste is treated only as a part of a binary relation. The rubbish producer is compelled to become a consumer of waste-management services.[12] The other instance occurs when rubbish is not included in this binary relation and is instead treated as a resource. It is not surprising that many of the most advanced systems of recycling, innovative rubbish treatment and the ability to use a loss as a resource function in urban slums.[13] Slum dwellers cannot afford to simply throw away things that can be preserved for further use. They cannot waste time or space if it can be made use of. Paying for organized rubbish collection would be a similar squander. People who live on resalable rubbish found in dumpsters in urban areas of developed countries are another example of this.[14] They can virtually support themselves relying only on things (mainly recyclable materials) which other city dwellers deem disposable. These two cases are not presented here to glorify social exclusion or enchant individual marginalization of a 'poor man'. Instead it is about the fact that mechanisms of using a loss are already present on the level of everyday practices, and as such they could be put to wider use.

## Connection attempts

Despite the two above-mentioned examples, general mechanisms of utilizing loss and breaking with the production-consumption paradigm are so far not available, partly because they would have to be locally reappropriated. However, conditions

---

12  Garth Myers, *African Cities: Alternative Visions of Urban Theory and Practice* (London: Zed Books, 2011), 33–34.

13  Jac Smit and Joe Nasr, 'Urban Agriculture for Sustainable Cities: Using Wastes and Idle Land and Water Bodies as Resources', *Environment and Urbanization* 4, no. 2 (1992): 141–52; Diana Lee-Smith, 'Cities Feeding People: An Update on Urban Agriculture in Equatorial Africa', *Environment and Urbanization* 22, no. 2 (2010): 483–99.

14  T. Rakowski, *Łowcy, zbieracze, praktycy niemocy. Etnografia człowieka zdegradowanego* [*Hunters, Gatherers, Practitioners of Feebleness: An Ethnography of Degraded Man*] (Gdańsk: Słowo/Obraz Terytoria, 2009).

for a possible three-part relation can be provisionally deter-mined. If we accept that re-industrialization is a tool, we need to think about the application of a loss/surplus in the urban con-text. Additionally, we need to consider to what extent mecha-nisms of loss have socially inclusive potential.

Getting access to traditional production processes on the level of organized creation (i.e. above the individual level, such as being an employee) is rather complicated and requires the overcoming of existing dependencies, e.g. technological, insti-tutional or political barriers. Personal involvement in the pro-duction process in the form of becoming a worker is also not relevant, because it does not transform the general situation. Opening a brewery in Camden or a cheese factory in Brook-lyn is surely nice, but has it any wider impact on the capitalist mode of production based on the production-consumption du-alism? The worker swiftly becomes a consumer, and the other way around, while being caught up in the reproduction of the conditions of his or her own dependency, which are constantly reinforced in colonized daily life.[15] Exploiting resources gener-ated by loss means breaking with this dialectical opposition and doing it with means already available. The worker/consumer is not compelled to struggle over traditional means of production, for his or her strength lies elsewhere — in the control over a loss/surplus.

It is difficult to imagine a circular production system which on the one hand would be able to fully make use of the losses it produces and on the other maintain an entry gate allowing for the inclusion of external elements. Such a system would be doomed either to authoritarian subjection of all elements of cir-culation or to a utopian (in the traditional meaning) and petri-fied autarky.

Recognizing the value of a loss is a condition of its social control and responsiveness towards new circumstances and needs. This social control is a crucial and critical element, be-

---

15   Henri Lefebvre, *Critique of Everyday Life,* vol. 3, trans. G. Elliott (London: Verso, 2008), 26.

cause it could form a mechanism preventing the seizure of loss by either production or consumption and by slipping to old divisions. It would also counteract the rule of internalization of profits and externalization of costs, which is essential for modern capitalism. This system is increasingly unable to manage surplus, understood both as consumer goods and as unwanted by-products. Mechanisms of loss, namely apprehension and social control of surplus, open possibilities for emancipation and for complication of capitalist functions.[16] Therefore, possible change lies not in the policies which would, for instance, enforce high fees for dumping waste in peripheral regions. That means at most giving poor countries a choice about a preferred form of subordination.[17] Recognition of the importance of loss for the socio-economic system and treating it as a manageable resource implies a shift in the power relations. The moment of power is relocated: hitherto weaker actors become decisive in the usage of loss/surplus. For instance, the development of digital technologies (mainly mobile phone applications, mobile banking and communication networks) in African countries is not a result of external capital or infrastructural investment, but innovative and productive ways of using computers and handsets deemed worthless by citizens of the developed countries.[18]

In the urban context, re-industrialization equals reformulation of spatial relations. Perhaps it is time now to think about something that could be called 'the architecture of loss'? Probably in the perspective of social control over the space right in the city is also to be practically reformulated. The starting point would be a practical reformulation of the 'right to the city' concept from the perspective of social control over space. On a low-

---

16 See the reconceptualization of city politics and policies in Edgar Pieterse, *City Futures: Confronting the Crisis of Urban Development* (London: Zed Books, 2008), 85–89.

17 Steven Graham and Simon Marvin, *Splintering Urbanism: Networked Infrastructures, Technological Mobilities and the Urban Condition* (London: Routledge, 2001), 304–78.

18 Anon., 'Press 1 for Modernity', *The Economist*, April 28, 2012, http://www. economist.com/node/21553510.

er and more important level, processes of industrial production are related to the material practices of people, their activities in and contacts with the environment. Possible social control over loss can be compared to the dominance over fragments of space, which, in spite of their crucial position for the functioning of the system, are currently understood as a burden, unless they can be subjugated and commodified. If the right to the city is a right to a social production of livable space, which in turn allows the individual and communal creation of reality,[19] then the key condition of its realization does not mean becoming a producer or a consumer. Rather it means recreating and taking advantage of available resources, such as losses, remainders, voids. The dialectical overcoming of productive or consumptive loss means constant creation of renewable resources. Loss/surplus is continuously produced by both practices of everyday life (i.e. most of people's activities in a city) and by industrial production. Therefore, re-industrialization should be comprehended as a social process containing and being contained by totality, but one without a center[20] It means going through different levels, understanding and inducing change which includes both general systemic importance and even people's minuscule material practices and their justifications.

It is not an attempt to determine the hard core of human identity (exemplified by the worker/consumer). It cannot be if we consider how inexhaustible the forms of people's productivity can be. It is rather about facilitating individual and social potential for shaping relations of production and consumption. By using existing resources and preserving the world as we know it, it is possible to change it completely.

---

19  Lefebvre, 'Right to the City', 147–59.
20  Jason Edwards, 'The Materialism of Dialectical Materialism', in *New Materialisms: Ontology, Agency and Politics*, eds. D. Coole and S. Frost (Durham: Duke University Press, 2010), 286.

# Chapter 3

# The Cultural Politics of Re-Industrialization
## Some Remarks on Cultural Policy and Urban Policy in the European Union

*Jonathan Vickery*

Cultural policy and urban policy in the European Union are two quite distinct policy fields. They overlap insofar as 'culture' is more often than not both urban and public culture, and the greatest density of publicly-funded cultural projects in Europe take place in cities. In this chapter I discuss how both cultural policy and urban policy are changing and are contributing to the ongoing need for re-industrialization, in part through providing the means to a new (or renewed) vision for the European city.

Europe experienced the de-industrialization of its post-war economy in the 1970s, then emerged a partial re-industrialization through a rising service economy in the liberalization of trade and property ownership in the 1980s, then to be followed by the informational, communications or so-called 'micro-chip revolution' of the 1990s — giving us the digitally-mediated economic world we today inhabit. And yet historical periodizations do not explain a great deal. How we conceptualize the meaning of 'industry' in the digital and so-called 'knowledge economy' of the present time remains a matter of debate, if not confusion, We currently seem to be living through an endless recessionary re-scaling of national economies within a supra-national European economic framework that is attempting to re-negotiate its relation to the global economy at the same time as its management of the grand political settlement of European unity, decisively forged at Maastricht in 1993. This will no doubt play out through successive political negotiations in the next decade or more, as Europe struggles to recover from the global financial crisis that impacted it in 2007.

In 2013, the EU arrived at the end of its last seven-year policy cycle (largely conceived before the European financial crisis fully emerged) and forthcoming strategic development frameworks—'Europe 2020' being the 'growth strategy'—are all confronting challenges greater than anything the Union has hitherto faced.[1] In this context, I will discuss the matter of policy with reference to 'Creative Europe' (the new cultural policy) and the somewhat less specific but equally significant policy term, 'integrated sustainable urban development'.

Even though it legislates, the EU is not a government, and so its political will is heavily invested in its policy discourse. While the EU's spectrum of competencies historically revolve around the governance of economy and trade, it now encompasses a range of rights and social values, supra-national political institutions and an increasing geo-political identity. 'The European Spatial Development Perspective' is, notionally at least, its largest framework for geo-social planning. This 'perspective' embodies related policy aspirations for territorial cohesion and regional integration, the cultural implications of which seem to contradict the 'principle of subsidiarity' enshrined at Maastricht. In one sense, EU cultural policy and urban policy both fall victim to the principle of subsidiarity (a member state's right to act outside the Union in certain areas), but in another sense,

---

1   European Commission, EUROPE 2020: A Strategy for Smart, Sustainable and Inclusive Growth (Brussels: Publications Office of the European Union, 2010).

subsidiarity motivates an ever greater need for a convincing policy unity. As articulated in the two treatises of the European Union, (which along with various additions are now considered in one 'consolidated' document), subsidiarity in principle is absolute but in practice must be interpreted within the priority of the ever expanding field of EU legal jurisdiction.[2]

Arguably, the most visible and recent EU discourse of re-industrialization revolves around the 'knowledge economy' concept, which can be understood less as a response to the rise of technology and the industrialization of science than as a permutation of the *entrepreneurial city* that emerged out of the widespread de-industrialization of the 1970s. The entrepreneurial city, as Bob Jessop explains, is not just a city with a competitive industrial infrastructure.[3] It is a city in which 'competitive advantage' is a hegemonic political discourse, which has re-structured the political complexion of the State, its services and welfare, urban space and social institutions, civil society and markets. This re-structuring has taken place around normative assumptions on the fundamental role of 'the economy' and how only market-driven economies are possess the energy and developmental potential to provide a stable ground for, and productive means to, animate and perpetuate a healthy society. Further, the entrepreneurial city as manifest in Europe has convincingly embodied a symbolic (and creative) articulation of

---

2   See: European Commission, *Committee on Spatial Development, European Spatial Development Perspective: Towards Balanced and Sustainable Development of the Territory of the European Union* (Luxembourg: Office for Official Publications of the European Communities, 1999). The two principal treaties are Treaty on the Functioning of the European Union (since 1958) and Treaty on European Union (i.e. the Maastricht Treaty, 1993); they were last updated at Lisbon (2009), whereupon the Charter of Fundamental Rights became legally binding. See European Union, *The Consolidated Treaties [and] Charter of Fundamental Rights* (Luxembourg: Publications Office of the European Union, 2010). This document cites 'subsidiarity' but also the 'harmonization of the laws and regulations of the Member States' (Article 167, 121–122).

3   Bob Jessop, 'The Entrepreneurial City', in *Transforming Cities: Contested Governance and New Spatial Divisions*, eds. N. Jewson and S. MacGregor, 28–41 (London: Routledge, 1997).

civic identity, where even heritage or abandoned factories become sites for aspirant innovative actors in the fast-changing
global economy. Renewal, regeneration and innovation are the
marks of the entrepreneurial city, whose techniques range from
dissolving the public ownership of welfare services, land and
property, to the use of the arts, culture and heritage to build a
branded visitor economy with extensive corporate hospitality
capability.[4]

The challenge for a critique of the entrepreneurial city, is that
its 'entrepreneurship' (and subsequent 'neoliberal' approach to
development) has been startlingly effective in giving culture,
arts and heritage a substantive socio-economic role in the urban
economy of the European city. In most European countries, the
so-called 'cultural sector' is now larger than it ever has been,
with impressive facilities and routine public funding. There
is little political solidarity among the European cultural elites
against a neoliberal regime that offers culture a lucrative role in
the contemporary city. For it does so without divesting it of its
historic (and hard-won) social autonomy, at least immediately.

This situation, however, is deceptive, and arguably retrenches
'autonomous' cultural sectors in politically marginalized social
spaces whose only function is to perpetuate a model of the city
it has received by fiat, and not to which it has imaginatively contributed. My argument, however, is that entrepreneurial neoliberal urban development has invoked a critical tension within
policy development at EU level. For the EU policy imaginary
must contend with the political conditions of its own legitimacy,
emerging from its own historicity, as well as offer an economically pragmatic and viable future for all its member states. I will
attempt to indicate how the EU's changing policy frameworks
articulate the political necessity of moving beyond the assumptions on the efficacy of corporate expansion and markets on
which the entrepreneurial city is founded.. The EU cannot fa-

---

4    Graeme Evans, 'Creative Cities, Creative Spaces and Urban Policy', *Urban
     Studies* 46, no. 5–6 (2009): 1003–40; Anne Lorentzen, 'Cities in the Experi-
     ence Economy', *European Planning Studies* 17, no. 6 (2009): 829–45.

cilitate the propulsion of its member-state cities into the global economy and endure what it calls the 'zero-sum' game of unrestrained competition between member state cities, between cities and regions, and city-regions with each other.[5]

For both urban policy and cultural policy, the EU was only really met with substantive enthusiasm from independent organizations, associations and city municipalities themselves, not national governments—for example, since 1951 the Council of European Municipalities and Regions (CEMR) and since 1986 EUROCITIES, have both played important roles in facilitating the credibility of EU policy. As by far the smaller of the two policy fields, cultural policy presides over a portfolio featuring education and media as well as the arts, culture, heritage, (and increasingly, the creative industries). Responsible for many high visibility projects (like the European Capital of Culture program) its success is largely judged by its central strategic funding project, formerly called the 'Culture Programme (2007–2013)'.[6] Having reached the end of its seven-year lifespan in 2013, the program had three objectives: cultural mobility, intercultural dialogue and the distribution of cultural goods (all geared to the central EU Treatises' aim of promoting the European polity through citizenship). It had a budget of €400 million and funded hundreds of projects, many of which had an urban dimension, such as the innovative project, House for Open Mobility Exchange (HOME) for 'personal contact in public spaces', and the BelBoBru 'urban parade laboratory'.[7] Impressive as the Programme was, its dis-

---

5   The phrase 'zero sum' is used in European Commission, *Cities of Tomorrow: Challenges, Visions, Ways Forward* (Luxembourg: Publications Office of the European Union, 2011), 22.

6   Culture is one of areas of the Directorate-General (DG) Education and Culture, the others include education and training, youth, sport, languages and media. The 'Cultural Programme (2007–13)' is one of seven programmes, some of which are relatively small (like the EU Culture Prizes, or the European Capital of Culture, which despite being a flagship programme has little funding attached).

7   European Commission, *Culture in Motion: The Culture Programme (2007-2013)* (Luxembourg: Communications Office of the European Union, 2010); see also European Commission, *Crossing Borders — Connecting Cul-*

crete range of projects and events (it did not fund individuals or places) only seemed to highlight the politically insular world of the European cultural elites, as if European cultural space is a parallel universe to national cultural sectors, and more so to the cultural life of rural and local communities.

Since 2000 and the largely over-optimistic 'Lisbon Agenda'—aiming to make the EU 'the most dynamic and competitive knowledge-based economy in the world by 2010' (a policy framework that exhibits the direct influence of Manuel Castells as well as Richard Florida)—cultural funding has been distributed outside the confines of the cultural sector, in industry and innovation schemes.[8] These schemes, arguably like the UK's 'culture-led regeneration' phenomena, utilized culture as an 'instrument' within a broader set of non-cultural objectives. The new 'European Agenda for Culture' (2007), however, shifted the gear of cultural policy.[9] While the initial 'Communication on a European Agenda for Culture in a Globalizing World' (2007) re-stated a commitment to national subsidiarity, it nonetheless asserted the *historically* international character of 'European culture' as a profound unity, and that economic growth now depends on digital connectivity, globalized markets and the distribution of cultural goods, which all now exceed national policy frameworks. There is a strong sense in which new urban and cultural policy is being bolstered in the face of intra-European

tures: *The EU Culture Programme (2007–2013)* (Brussels: Publications Office of the European Union, 2011). For cited projects, see 'Other Projects,' *LUGD* [website], http://www.ljud.si/slo/?page_id= 10&lang=en, and http://newnostradamusofthenorth.blogspot.co.uk/2011/05/celebrating-variety-of-eu-taxpayer.html (original website now expired)

8   The 'Lisbon Agenda' action and development plan (2000), for the EU economy between 2000 and 2010. See Arno Tausch, *Titanic 2010: The European Union and Its Failed Lisbon Strategy* (Hauppauge: Nova Science Publishers, 2010).

9   European Commission, *European Agenda for Culture in a Globalizing World* (Brussels: Publications Office of the European Union, 2007), 2-3. See also the accompanying document on policy implementation: European Commission, *Working Document: The European Agenda for Culture — Progress towards Shared Goals* (Brussels: Publications Office of the European Union, 2007).

competition and against member states' particularist planning trajectories.

The new cultural program is 'Creative Europe' (2014–2020). The budget was agreed upon in 2011, adjusted downwards due to recessionary pressures, but still now stands as an almost 10% increase at a substantial €1.46 billion.[10] It is structurally different to its predecessor in two crucial ways: it merges funding for culture and media (the previous Culture and MEDIA and MEDIA Mundus programs); and positions the commercial creative industries as co-extensive with 'culture', further opening cultural projects to industrial innovation and scientific funding collaborations. The first of these is significant in view of the established debate and frustrated pan-European attempts to develop a European public sphere.[11] The second is significant in that culture has explicitly been positioned within economic development, and this seems to have come at the cost of the traditional aim of EU cultural policy—European citizenship. The new policy emphasis for culture as economic stimulus sees culture as the mobilization of a young, flexible, mobile and largely a-political workforce for either new enterprise or corporate expansion through innovation. The new aims of cultural policy feature a repetitive use of the lexicon of economic growth — globalization, employment and markets.

On the face of it, the new central policy program for culture may seem like an attempt to dissolve the hegemony of the traditional institutions of culture in favor of a new EU-wide dynamic culture *industry,* driven by 'creative' industries' models of development (itself driven by American models of business entrepreneurship). The culture program offers Bank Loan Guarantees

10  European Commission, *Creative Europe: The European Union Programme for the Cultural and Creative Sectors (2014–2020)* (Brussels: Publications Office of the European Union, 2011), 786/2

11  Of the many EU-sponsored studies of the so-called 'European public sphere', see: H.G. Sicakkan, *Diversity and the European Public Sphere towards a Citizens' Europe.* EUROSPHERE Final Comparative Study, vol. 3 (2013), http://eurosphere.uib.no/files/2010/07/EUROSPHERE_Final-Report_Web_version2.pdf.

for SMES (Small and Medium-sized Enterprises) managed by the European Investment Fund (EIF), and so for the first time the cultural and the banking sectors become interconnected. And yet, the 2010 European Commission green paper *Unlocking the Potential of Cultural and Creative Industries* (2010) did not appeal to the EU's Enterprise and Industry policy field, but to cultural policy itself.[12] Culture's 'autonomy' is actually prized in the face of the apparent instrumentalist orientation of culture to economy. Creative Europe, it seems, indeed exhibits all the elements of New Economic Growth Theory, with its talk of cross-sector partnerships and service-based administration methods, clusters and incubators, and a capitalization on so-called 'crossover effects'. Yet again, it is assertive in valuing culture on its own terms and of artistic or aesthetic experience as a significant realm of meaning as much as social benefit. EU policies cannot simply be understood as a series of statements or directives issued from discrete documents. Policy in the EU is a political imaginary, where a vision of a distinctive European society is required to safeguard the authority and legitimacy of the 'managers' of this society (the EU as democratic polity).

The inextricable interconnection of the cultural and the urban at the level of policy was made apparent by Richard Florida's 2004 study of European countries, *Europe in the Creative Age*.[13] Ironically, cities themselves did not feature large in his study, but Florida since remained a central figure in the development of the entrepreneurial city discourse across Europe. While ostensibly based on 'data', the 2004 study was tacitly animated by a demand that European policy makers reconcile themselves to a new 'creative age'. This 'age' sustained itself through economic growth, and growth was maintained through individual professional success, and a success that emerged through specialist education, skills and competitiveness, resulting in new enterprises

---

12 European Commission, *Unlocking the Potential of Cultural and Creative Industries* (Brussels: Publications Office of the European Union, 2010).

13 Richard Florida and Irene Tinagli, *Europe in the Creative Age* (London: Demos, 2004).

and cities bustling with enterprise-affected activity (more production, but also intensified consumption). The many official
EU events for the so-designated European Year of Creativity and
Innovation in 2009 articulated this logic very effectively, but in
two ways. The consequent and widely circulated *European Am-
bassadors for Creativity and Innovation Manifesto* (with Florida
as an 'ambassador') was cosmopolitan and in a general way located the conditions for such growth in the material-institution-
al environments of particular urban economies (which indeed
require a cognitive infrastructure of actual cultural creativity).
Other areas, like the 'cluster' discourse, emerged across Europe
and presented a more narrow investment in business enterprise
and innovation models (see the European Cluster Alliance, European Cluster Observatory, and others). Related streams of the
'Europe 2020' framework—like the 'Innovation Union'—along
with the new EU Small Business Act for Europe (2008), and EU
Strategy on Intellectual Property, could have served either, and
both strands could have complimented each other on the level of
practice. In policy terms, the narrow version of Florida's creative
age thesis has become dominant in many European countries
and for the most part simply promotes the economic agenda of
the old entrepreneurial city.[14]

And yet, the EU requires more than just operational effectiveness on the economic register; it requires the perpetual legitimacy of its increasingly complex governance, particularly in
current times of crisis. Reading across the major policy decla-
rations and directives on the urban policy and cultural policy
of the last two decades, one encounters the rhetoric of entrepreneurial economic growth for sure, yet also something else.
On the one hand urban policy is the locus of some of the most
compelling problems in technology and engineering (security,
renewable energy, transportation, and so on), and on the other
it remains animated by, and continues to respond to, the social
dilemmas that has faced European identity since its original

---

14 European Commission, *State of the Innovation Union 2012: Accelerating
Change* (Luxembourg: Publications Office of the European Union, 2013).

historic emergence (dilemmas of integration and a common culture, social welfare and equality). The same can be said for cultural policy.

Urban policy in the EU is a hybrid field with no actual basis in any treaty. There are relevant committees or representatives on urban matters in almost all of the EU's institutions, and some of its investment projects (such as the European Regional Development Fund: the ERDF). While managed in the broad context of Cohesion Policy, and as a specific investment arm of Regional Policy, the ERDF has played an increasingly significant policy role for culture — providing new spaces, places and facilities as part of broader urban development projects.[15] One of the most important policy developments, however, is actually not a policy at all. The 'European Acquis Urbain' (sometimes just referred to as the EU Urban Agenda) is is like the term 'Integrated Sustainable Urban Development' and acts as a meta-theory of EU urban policy implementation. While in practical terms, it articulates an understanding of urban policy that presents itself in terms of a strategic pragmatism accumulated through decades of practice. Philosophically, the Acquis Urbain is a significant counterweight to the continued enthusiasm for the 'Lisbon Agenda' for a knowledge economy (2000) — which was not backed by much statutory power in any case, but which has maintained the entrepreneurial lexicon of terms for many an urban policy maker interested in culture and creative industries.[16]

While the Cohesion Policy 2014–20 supports an 'integrated sustainable urban development' approach to all policy making

---

15 The European Regional Development Fund (ERDF), the Cohesion Fund and the European Social Fund are the three main financial instruments of EU Cohesion Policy (run by DG Regio). The Cohesion Policy for 2014–2020 contains new regulations to set out common objectives for all structural intervention (under the new mantra of 'smart, sustainable, and inclusive').

16 Successive informal ministerial meetings on urban development (in Lille in 2000, Rotterdam in 2004, Bristol in 2005, Leipzig in 2007, Marseille in 2008 and Toledo in 2010) shaped the common Acquis Urbain: the founding document is the 2003 Declaration of Strasbourg, influenced in no short measure by the Council of Europe's Urban Charter II in preparation at the time (ratified in 2008).

in principle, in reality it is mandatory only in small and specific areas (parts of ERDF spending). There remains an apparent problem: policies on urban life are a vast field for which a
vision of a re-industrialized city is not a specific model of city
planning.[17] Nonetheless, the Acquis Urbain is as much a rejection of the economic instrumentalism of the UK model of 'urban
regeneration' as it is the narrow Florida-style entrepreneurial
economy (and its recent reincarnation in the 'Smart City'). For
while economy and business remain emphatic in EU urban policy, they are not internal to development itself, and not a condition of sustainability as such. This can be seen in part in the
adopted EU Sustainable Development Strategy (SDS) of 2006,
the 2007 'Leipzig Charter on Sustainable European Cities' and
up to the brochure-style publications like *Promoting Sustainable
Urban Development in Europe* (2009), and particularly the in-
spirational *Cities of Tomorrow: Challenges, Visions, Ways Forward* (2011).[18] The elements of New Economic Growth Theory
are present, but taken as 'given', albeit meaningless without a
greater strategic European vision for social change. And this vision is articulated in a way that is ideologically incontestable, as
it draws on the originary European Union political philosophy
of equitable pan-national social welfare, where development is
most fundamentally a form of socio-cultural participation, and
sustainability is a non-negotiable ethic of everyday life.

Of course, one could easily retort that this above vision is
little more than the old traditional European statism, reliant on
national monocultural allegiances, a heavy industrial base and
high taxation, which were all the reasons for Europe's economic
decline. However, this is not the case; what I am identifying here
is not a battle between two ideologies or state systems, but the

---

17  See European Commission, *Inter-Service Group on Urban Development: The
    Urban Dimension in European Union Policies 2010, Introduction and Part 1:
    European Commission* (Brussels: Publications Office of the European Un-
    ion, 2010).

18  European Commission, *Promoting Sustainable Urban Development in Eu-
    rope: Achievements and Opportunities* (Brussels: Publications Office of the
    European Union, 2009); European Commission, *Cities of Tomorrow*.

fact of a strategic contention between two complex discourses, both of which retain a profound dimension of necessity. The entrepreneurial neoliberal city and the historic (if evolving) 'European' city are not exclusive. It is their perplexing mutual interconnection that has, at least in part, motivated the huge and increasing need for research, addressing an acute deficit in theoretical understanding.

It is the Acquis Urbain that articulates this most vividly, with its call for knowledge. Required is the knowledge generated from actual practice — urban development itself is a knowledge-generating activity. Embedded knowledge gathering (what it calls an 'urban methodology') can be generated out of actual place-based engagements, where these take place on the basis of the socio-cultural or 'European' orientation of the Acquis Urbain. This has been done to some degree in past urban development with the Urban Pilot Projects (1989–99) and the URBAN and URBAN II Community Initiatives (1994–2006) and the URBACT program (2002–13: the acronyms of EU such projects, which having their source in benign terms like 'urban actions', are now established and strategically managed cultural brands). The URBACT strategic funding instrument has been exemplary in its demonstration of the need to understand the complexity of urban culture as a prerequisite to infrastructural design and construction, and other forms of development. The seminal statement on integration, *Towards an Urban Agenda in the European Union* (1997), proclaimed that urban policy was to 'restore the role of Europe's cities as places of social and cultural integration, as sources of economic prosperity and sustainable development, and as the bases of democracy.'[19]

The term 'integrated', in Integrated Sustainable Urban Development, tacitly confronts the disciplinary basis of national urban policy practices in parochial town- or city-planning traditions, the hegemonic discourse of 'planning' over urban development, and with it the domination of traditional civil engineer-

---

19 European Commission, *Towards an Urban Agenda in the European Union* (Brussels: Publications Office of the European Union, 1997), 3.

ing or industrial engineering ways of thinking over planning). If development emerges from knowledge construction, and not simply a hoped for 'effect' of market forces, then 'sustainability' is a means of activating an evolving historicity. Rescued from the political discourse of energy consumption and taxation so favored by national governments, 'sustainability' is becoming a marker for a vast realm of academic (and so, policy) ignorance on the relation between the urban and the natural environment.

It is the visionary document *Cities of Tomorrow* (2011) that fleshes some of this out. The document approvingly reproduces a piece of Berlin graffiti, demanding we 'stop gentrification', yet the need for industry and business are no less rigorously understood. Both are positioned in this policy discourse within 'advanced social progress', as 'platforms for democracy, cultural dialogue and diversity' and as participating in the creation of 'places of green, ecological or environmental regeneration'.[20] The term 'smart' is used frequently (to define specialized research and technology-based innovations), but only in relation to its social conditions of 'inclusive' opportunity and equity. The European city of tomorrow will exhibit 'limited urban sprawl through a strong control of land supply and speculative development'.[21] It is driven by new political alliances of engaged independent representation, with legitimate roles for city-based civil society, NGOs and new urban actors. In short, in the European city of tomorrow, the economic — not the urban or cultural — is burdened with the task of defining itself and delivering on the social and political demands of a new EU city polity.

My purpose in this chapter was to indicate the changing complexion and interrelation of cultural policy and urban policy. The need for re-industrialization has demanded that each policy framework adopt the lexicon of, and orientation towards, economic development. This has generated a dilemma for these European Union policy fields, and this dilemma is manifest in a significant structural tension. While to define this structural

---

20  European Commission, *Cities of Tomorrow*, 10.
21  Ibid., 12.

tension in terms of a contradiction would be to collapse our understanding of a complex process into a reductive choice between opposites. Rather, the tension is the visible struggle of the EU policy imaginary that is undergoing a necessary intellectual as well as political negotiation. This negotiation is between the raison d'être of the historical European democratic polity and the requirements of prosperity in a market-driven global economy. It is a quest for an integrated sustainable development and it is hanging in the balance.

# Chapter 4

# 'Shrimps not Whales'
# Building a City of Small Parts as
# an Alternative Vision for
# Post-Industrial Society

*Alison Hulme*

I was expecting the necessity of a protracted explanation on my part as to where exactly I wanted to go, but the taxi driver immediately knew, despite the fact that 798 Art District is way up in the northeast of Beijing, adjacent to a nondescript business centre in what was a German military camp enclosure. It is no longer enclosed. It no longer needs to be. The government has long ago seen the sense in accessibility and careful encouragement where art is concerned, as strategies to avoid secrecy and dissent by potentially counter-revolutionary artists and intellectuals.

Passing under the industrial, red iron gatepost into the plain, wide street, with its red-brick ex-military buildings on either side, an old, rusting, water-pipe juts out into the pavement, spluttering and spurting through its seams. It is tempting to think these industrial remnants have no function whatsoever and have simply been left to provide the effect of things being make-shift. The huge iron doors of the gallery spaces, rusting and squeaking on their hinges, are part of the same visual rhetoric, as is the content-less graffiti — all so carefully disheveled. There is nothing make-shift about 798 any longer, and the price of the food in the various café spaces, complete with their distressed furniture, is proof that shabby-chic *bo-bo*[1] style sells.

Later, a local Beijinger tells me that 798 is one of the most profitable local neighborhoods of Beijing — not far behind the central touristic areas containing Tiananmen Square and the Summer Palace, or the corporate business areas. This is not altogether surprising; 'bringing in the artists' has long been a way to regenerate run-down urban areas in Western cities and neatly fits the rhetoric surrounding 'the creative city' promulgated by the likes of Richard Florida.[2] It is also almost immediately hijackable by neoliberal agendas (if not created with them in mind from the outset), whose concern is property prices and ABC1 consumers.[3] Indeed, the 'creative city' has seemingly become the only answer to post-industrial urban stagnancy — reindustrialization is off the agenda.

In many ways, utilizing the art world or 'creatives' to regenerate specific areas of a city can be seen as part of what Brenner and Theodore call the 'embedded-ness of neo-liberalism', by which they mean the way in which neoliberalism is produced and defined by inherited frameworks, as opposed to simply using (allegedly) immutable market forces wherever they decide

---

1   'Bourgeois Bohemian'.

2   Richard Florida, *The Rise of the Creative Class: And How It's Transforming Work, Leisure, Community and Everyday Life* (New York: Perseus Book Group, 2002); R. Florida, *Cities and the Creative Class* (New York: Routledge, 2005). Florida's thesis states that there is a creative class who are a key driving force for economic development of post-industrial cities in the US. He breaks the class into a 'super-creative' core consisting of science, engineering, education, computer programming, research, arts, design and media workers, and a group of 'creative professionals' who are the classic knowledge-based workers, including those in healthcare, business and finance, the legal sector and education.

3   This relates to the first three categories of the accepted social grade definitions used by the market and social research industry in the UK. They aim to measure and classify people by income and earnings levels. The full scale of definitions runs from A to E, A being higher managerial, administrative or professional workers, and E being casual or lowest-grade workers.

to unleash them.[4] They draw upon the work of Peck and Tickell, who have emphasized the way in which neoliberalization is a *process* — an on-going movement of destruction and creation at the local, national and global level.[5] The encouragement of art districts to gentrify run-down areas is precisely the utilization of neoliberal logic in order to re-appropriate an often alternative space into something that fits its own agenda whilst maintaining the outward appearance of being 'different' and 'independent'. It is, perhaps without realizing it itself, 'path-dependent' in other words, and that path in the late twentieth and early twenty-first centuries has seen creative industries usurp traditional manufacturing as part of an increasingly embedded lineage of neoliberalism. The question then becomes, how to break the path?

***

Far from Beijing 798, lies the 'small commodities' city of Yiwu, in Zhejiang province. Via its prolific manufacturing of low-end goods (batteries, plastic-wear, decorative trinkets), it has gone from being a small village to a hugely successful driver of regional growth. The 'Yiwu model' has even been copied and exported to other countries — Dubai, The Netherlands and Sweden, for example. Its raison d'être can most evidently be seen in its lay-out, which centers around the immense wholesale markets, housed in giant warehouses and zoned according to commodity. The Yiwu model was inspired by 'Zhejiang Village' (Zhejiangcun), a migrant clothing manufacturing area in the Fengtai district of Beijing. Despite (or perhaps because of) its success, 1995 saw the complete razing of Zhejiangcun, causing a mass exodus of around 40,000 migrants. In its place the

---

4   Neil Brenner and Nik Theodore, 'Cities and the Geographies of "Actually Existing Neoliberalism"', in *Spaces of Neoliberalism: Urban Restructuring in North America and Western Europe,* eds. Neil Brenner and Nik Theodore, 2–32 (Oxford: Blackwell Publishing, 2002).

5   Jamie Peck and Adam Tickell, "Neoliberalising Space", *Antipode* 34, no.3 (2002): 380–404, at 380.

authorities built an enormous modern plaza — deemed to be a more 'suitable' representation of the new China.

Zhejiangcun was characterized by four key features attributed to its migrants' former practices in their native city of Wenzhou, Zhejiang Province, and these characteristics have informed and remained constant in Yiwu. They were: (1) that it consisted of numerous small-scale private enterprises, (2) that it specialized in wholesale petty commodity markets, (3) that it was built on tens of thousands of mobile traders who facilitated the flow of materials and (4) that it was made possible by various forms of non-governmental financial arrangements.[6] These characteristics had become known as the 'Wenzhou model', a phrase which was officially announced as a new economic paradigm for China in 1986. Despite this, versions of the model that did not have the right 'look' were clearly unacceptable.

The fact that Wenzhou had created the model was not simply coincidence, but also a result of its historical ties with the Yongjia school of thought — a movement from Yongjia County in the Wenzhou region, whose roots lie in the Southern Song Dynasty. The school contested the view of mainstream Confucianism, arguing that traders (as well as scholars and farmers) were the backbone of the country. So, unlike in other provinces where under Confucianism land was valorized and peoples' attachment to it revered, in Wenzhou commercialism had been celebrated historically. This all changed of course under Mao, who was specifically against small-scale enterprises, as he felt that industry at the level of the family unit was particularly open to 'spontaneous capitalistic urges'. Deng Xiao Ping, however, under the rhetoric of re-appropriating neo-Confucianism to encourage small business start-ups, proclaimed the Wenzhou model as that which China should adopt. So, after a long and embattled history, the Wenzhou model gained official acceptance — as long, that is, as it cleaned up its act and started to con-

---

6   Li Zhang, *Strangers in the City: Reconfigurations of Space, Power, and Social Networks within China's Floating Population* (Stanford: Stanford University Press, 2001), 52–53.

form to the 'look' deemed appropriate to a modern 'civilized' China.

\*\*\*

My reason for drawing upon these two seemingly unrelated examples is to underline the way in which different Chinese authorities are drawing upon very different 'answers' — one borrowed from the West, the other entirely home-grown. The home-grown Wenzhou model can be seen, in some ways, as a modus operandi similar to (and this is certainly not to suggest that it is based on) Britain's pre- or proto-industrial past. The 798 Art District model is adapted directly from our own current practices of urban regeneration. What I am arguing here is that it may be the model from the past, but in its current Chinese form it has the most to offer us when we think about how we can improve our own cities in a manner more able to avoid the usual neoliberal traps. 'Returning' to a form of proto-industrialization, but one adapted to our current socio-political needs, has the added benefit of breaking the current processes of neoliberalization in place. It perhaps provides an answer to my earlier question — it is a path-breaker.

The feature of the Wenzhou model that is key here is its small-scale nature — the way in which it is based on numerous small-scale enterprises, rather than the 'big capitalism' we now have in the West. This is a phenomenon that Chinese entrepreneur Jack Ma[7] once described as being concerned with 'shrimps not whales'. It can usefully be compared to what we in the West

---

7   Jack Ma is a famous business entrepreneur in China. He owns the highly successful business-to-business website, Taobao, the Chinese equivalent to eBay, and is the Alan Sugar figure on China's version of the television show *The Apprentice*. In a 2000 interview for *Time Asia* magazine he explained the thinking behind Taobao, saying, 'American B2B sites are whales. But 85% of the fish in the sea are shrimp-sized. I don't know anyone who makes money from whales, but I've seen many making money from shrimp'. See *Time* staff, 'Jack Ma', *Time* (February 28, 2000), http://content.time.com/time/world/article/0,8599,2054856,00.html.

call the 'cottage industry'. Most importantly, the cottage industry is specifically related to workers operating *according to their
own preferences,* as independent entities who own their means
of production. The era of the cottage industry, sometimes referred to as 'proto-industrialization', soon emerged into an era
of industrialization in Britain, whereas in China it has had a far
more continuous trajectory, finding form in all eras apart from
the Maoist one. In addition, 'small business' was never the official paradigm in Britain, nor was it given the legitimation of a
cultural tradition such as neo-Confucianism was. Therefore, the
means of organizing witnessed in the proto-industrial phase, i.e.
'cottage industries', have a greater continuity in China and have
found their way into the economic structures of the twenty-first
century. China is in fact a country where a capitalism of many
small parts exists alongside big capitalism (both domestic and
international).

With this in mind, it may indeed be worth considering re-
industrialization as an answer to the crisis we face in Western
cities, but not re-industrialization as we tend to imagine it. This
re-industrialization would need to be one which, from its incep-
tion and at its philosophical core, was of shrimps not whales. In
order to be a progressive socio-political and economical project
that could operate differently, or outside of, the neoliberal city
as we know it, it would need to be committed to its parts remaining small-scale and not requiring high profit margins. Of
course, it would also need to limit its reliance upon wider global
economic machinations, which would probably mean implementing a form of mutual finance amongst those involved. In
addition, it would need to go beyond 'boutique manufacturing',
using the same logic of production for everyday and creative
(perhaps non-tangible) products. Re-claiming/claiming urban
space would be a huge part of this initiative if the existing structural order were to be overcome. Mutual systems of space would
be required which would enable life/work situations, both in
run-down areas but also eventually in the centers of cities usually inaccessible as living spaces to all but the super-rich.

It is the re-ordering of space and structures which makes a Western urban version of the Wenzhou model attractive. It is, indeed, a new model, not simply a creative industry being encouraged within the parameters of existing neoliberal capitalism. It can be seen as a re-invention of a form of production from our own past, but one that in learning from the Wenzhou model is able to operate in a way that does not mean we must regress to the kinds of jobs and working situations associated with earlier forms of manufacturing economy. Crucially, though, it must be able to exist contemporaneously with big capitalism. This will require some impressive tactics and a stoic resistance on the part of those adopting the model if they are to prove that an alternative model of 'shrimps not whales' can affectively function in twenty-first-century industrialized cities.

Chapter 5

# 'Der Arbeiter' (Re-)Industrialization as Universalism?

## Krzysztof Nawratek

In the first chapter of *The Urban Revolution,* Henri Lefebvre shows the evolution of the city — from the political city, through the mercantile and industrial city, to its final form, the true 'urban city'. For Lefebvre, industry is something that wasn't born in the city.

He asks: 'Was industry associated with the city?' And answers: 'One would assume it to be associated with the *non-city,* the absence or rupture of urban reality.'[1] It was the industry that came to the city, lured by the scent of money, and the sweat and blood of its inhabitants. However, Lefevbre's attitude towards the industrial city is dialectical. The industrial city destroyed the remnants of the mercantile city and the political city, but it was a 'creative destruction', which, in fact, elevated the city to a higher level of development, setting the stage for Lefebvre's 'critical zone', the predicted moment in history in which urbanity becomes a meta-narrative aligning all other stories, and therefore also includes the politics and economics of the city.

---

1     Henri Lefebvre, *The Urban Revolution* (Minneapolis: University of Minnesota Press, 2013), 13.

Chris Evans[2] describes life in Merthryr Tydfil in the nineteenth century at the beginning of the industrial revolution, where the first workers' strike broke out. Merthryr Tydfil was almost completely devoid of anything that is usually associated with the city — its only public building was a church, street lighting was installed only in the second half of the nineteenth century and the availability of goods and services was very poor (one store to 400 inhabitants, while the norm for British cities was about one to 100 and better). This un-urban city, which at that time was the centre of world industrial production, had no schools and no recreational areas or buildings.

Does the Merthryr Tydfil example (and other cities of the Industrial Revolution) provide sufficient evidence to support Henri Lefevbre's perspective of the non-urban character of industry? Let's go back to 'The Urban Revolution', where he describes the mechanism of the transition from the political city to the mercantile city. Trade and traders were kept out of cities politics; the city was autonomous, and their success was associated with being seen as 'free radicals' with effective mobility.

The position of trade and traders in the city brings to mind the distinction made by Carl Schmitt between 'the orders of the land' and of 'the sea'.[3] Schmitt associates 'the order of the sea' with liberal-democratic capitalism, mainly in the American edition, which involves both the freedom and the a-territoriality of trade, but even more so with the contemporary free movement of speculative capital.

Industry, which colonized and transformed the city, can be seen then as a free radical; however its existence was strongly associated with a particular spatial location. In a similar way, he mercantile city was founded when the trade was 'grounded' and traders became the townspeople/bourgeoisie). Industry and the

---

2   C. Evans, 'Merthryr Tyndif in the Eighteenth Century: Urban by Default', in *Industry and Urbanization in Eighteenth-century England,* eds. P. Clark and P. Corfield, 11–18 (Leicester: Leicester University Press, 1994).

3   S. Legg (ed.), *Spatiality, Sovereignty and Carl Schmitt: Geography of the Nomos* (London: Routledge, 2011).

industrial city are (were) then a spatial entity, belonging to the land order.

This implies that the industrial city was conservative, but its conservatism is understood here as a kind of slow development, providing predictability and a strengthening of the social structures, such as family or local community. This is the conservatism of Fordism and the welfare state (and thus the conservatism of Social Democrats and Christian Democrats, but not the radical — especially contemporary — neoliberal right). This is the same conservatism which was first dismantled by the New Left movements growing from the heritage of the May '68 movement (Henri Lefevbre's *The Urban Revolution* is obviously the result of May '68 and an important part of its legacy), and then by the conservative revolution of the 1980s and the excesses of neoliberalism. But let's go back to the first half of the twentieth century, to the time when the industrial city seemed to be the triumphant revolutionary change. Let's follow a guide to this imaginary and never-realized world: Ernst Jünger's *Der Arbeiter*.[4]

*Der Arbeiter* is an extraordinary book — one aspect of its uniqueness, for example, is the fact that it was never translated in full into English. Reading *Der Arbeiter* one may feel slightly confused — on the one hand, this book is considered to be a prophetic vision of modern society; on the other hand, it is difficult to forget that it was published a year before the Nazis came to power and that Jünger himself was associated with the intellectual circles of the German 'conservative revolution' of the Weimar Republic.

Despite the fact that it is difficult to directly associate the author with the Nazi regime, it is also not easy to consider him as a declared anti-fascist. It is important, though, to considerJünger's relationship with fringes of fascist ideas in the context of the

---

4  Ernst Jünger, *Der Arbeiter: Herrschaft und Gestalt* (Hamburg: Hanseatische Verlagsanstalt, 1941 [1932]). I have been using Polish edition: E. Jünger, *Robotnik: Panowanie i forma bytu* (Warsaw: PWN, 2010). All quotations refer to this edition.

industrial city, because the specificity of the economic structure of the Third Reich highlights crucial aspects of the industrial-city phenomenon. It shows that in fact it doesn't matter in what system the industrial city existed, whether it was the capitalist America or the communist Soviet Union. What distinguishes the industrial city is a kind of 'transcendent organicity'.

In his classic work, 'The structure of Nazi economy', Maxime Y. Sweezy [5] shows a fully capitalist economic structure, which could even be described as neoliberal. The Nazi economy was focused on the strengthening of the private capital (the 'Nazi privatization' as a prototype for contemporary neoliberal policies is described by Germa Bel),[6] and on the development of large-scale industry and agriculture at the expense of small family farms and businesses.

In the context of *Der Arbeiter*, Gehrard Schultz's opinion, expressed in the book *Die nationalsozialistiche Machtergreifung* is crucial: 'Instead of a number of economic objectives, the state has adopted one — a total mobilization of the entire nation for the total war'.[7] 'Total mobilization' is one of the key concepts thatJünger introduced to contemporary socio-political thought.[8] For the purpose of this text, the key observation concerns the location of the order-making and sense-giving structure to the industrial city which is external to the industrial city itself. I argue that the industrial city does not exist through industry only, but by giving it meaning beyond production.

5  Marine Sweezy, *The Structure of the Nazi Economy* (Cambridge: Harvard University Press, 1941).

6  Germà Bel, 'Against the Mainstream: Nazi Privatization in 1930s Germany', *The Economic History Review* 63, no. 1 (2010): 34–55.

7  Quoted in S. Ratner, 'An Inquiry into the Nazi War Economy', Review of *Design for Total War: Arms and Economics in The Third Reich,* by Bernice A. Carroll,' *Comparative Studies in Society and History* 12, no. 4 (1970): 466–72.

8  Ernst Jünger, 'Total Mobilisation', in *Krieg und Krieger* (Berlin: Junker und Dunnhaupt, 1930). Polish translation in: Wojciech Kunicki, *Rewolucja konserwatywna w Niemczech 1918–1933* (Poznań: Wydawnictwo Poznańskie, 1999); English translation available from: http://anarchistwithoutcontent. wordpress.com/2010/12/05/junger-total-mobilization/.

It is this 'transcendent' sense that constitutes the industrial city, rather than a mere presence of the industry in the city. This transcendent order was present in the form of the totalitarian structures of the Third Reich, the communism of war, the American New Deal and finally in the form of a welfare state as an attempt to build a truly inclusive and integrated society. The industrial city — similar to today's neoliberal city — was a result of a particular political vision based on certain values and ideas.

Jünger describes modern society as a work society, in which work is 'a form of being'. There is nothing that is not work, and there is no one who does not work. Work eliminates all differences and hierarchies: 'All the decisive mobilization orders do not run from the top down, but emerge as a revolutionary goal, making it more effective'.[9] Work eliminates democracy as a choice and replaces it with democracy as act — 'Acceptance takes place through pure participation, and therefore through the participation in voting, regardless of which party wins'[10] — and it challenges the privilege of individual freedom.

Interestingly, Jünger not only challenges the notion of the individual but also the mass (as a collection of individuals):

> The movements of the masses have lost their irresistible charm wherever they encounter strong resistance — as in two or three old soldiers behind a working machine gun [who] were not concerned with a report that they are being charged by a whole battalion. Mass today is incapable of charging, it is incapable even of defence.[11]

The idea of the worker (*Arbeiter*) seems totalistic, but it is an inclusive totality (I would like to make a distinction between 'totalistic' and 'totalitarian' and I would argue that Der Arbeiter does not praise totalitarianism): no one is excluded, because everyone is a part of the great totalistic machinery: 'Man is the

---

9   Jünger, *Robotnik*, 241.
10  Ibid., 240.
11  Ibid., 109.

source of natural wealth, and no state plan will ever be perfect unless it can draw from this source'[12] (in this context, of course, the Third Reich, with its master race ideology and concentration camps, is not a realization of Ernst Jünger's vision).

The world presented in *Der Arbeiter* is not the world of class or nation (although Jünger sees the Germans as the vanguard of the world), it is also not the world of profit and exploitation, asJünger writes, 'Private initiative will be acceptable when it obtains a status of a specialized type of work — in other words[,] when it is controlled within the broader process.'[13] It is a world of 'Plan' and 'Higher Purpose'. It is a world in which everything makes sense — control does not come 'from above', for there is no institutional Big Brother or any controlling authority — but it is through its very own logic of existence that this world gives itself meaning: 'Every movement of his hand, even while cleaning the stables from manure, has its rank, if it does not feel as an abstract work, but fits within [a] greater and sensible order.'[14]

Historians such as Hugh Trevor-Roper and Bernice A. Carroll (the author of Design for Total War),[15] conclude with surprise the lack of total control in the Third Reich economy, replaced by a totalitarian socio-political formation. And it is this 'external' control that appears to have the dominant role. So I agree with Lefevbre's observation of 'externality' of the agent of change to the city (whether it was trade or industry), but I disagree with the stipulated imminence of the 'ultimate form of the city' as something desirable. To some extent, the existing model of neoliberal urbanization is a nightmarish version of Lefevbre's vision. It's a nightmare because this vision is closed, and therefore dead.

Jünger's book begins with a discussion of the bourgeois attempt to suppress the Worker by shaping him in a bourgeois fashion. *Der Arbeiter* is a song about the world in which the bour-

---

12  Ibid., 272.
13  Ibid., 275.
14  Ibid., 281–82.
15  Berenice A. Carroll, *Design for Total War: Arms and Economics in the Third Reich* (The Hague: Mouton De Gruyter, 1968).

geoisie lost and the totality of work conquered all other logics. Our world is obviously not the world predicted byJünger — on the contrary, the Bourgeois defeated the Worker, debased and destroyed him. In this context, we can finally ask the question: Is the industrial city a dead idea too? Is re-industrialization just a fantasy of another time and another world?

The discussion about re-industrialization in Western Europe and the US began only a few years ago, when the 2008 crisis made obvious the bankruptcy of the model of urban development based on property speculation and liquid capitalism. Re-Industrialization can be defined in many ways and does not necessarily apply only to cities. That is why I would rather talked about the industrial city 2.0 — the 'comeback' of the industry to the cities is not crucial in itself; what's more important is the empowerment and embedding of the industry in the socio-economic structure of the city.

Using New York as an example, Sarah Crean[16] indicates the emerging networks between different actors involved in industrial production — from representatives of the 'creative class', like designers and engineers, through producers and finally consumers. Also, at the institutional level new networks emerge linking manufacturers, suppliers, distributors and consumers.

This feature of industrial production — creation of relationships — connects in an interesting way with today's obsession with networking and the social network. Creating relationships and systems of mutual dependency is the most important feature of contemporary thinking about industry and production based on 'industrial ecology' and 'circular economy'.

Production based on the idea of a 'circular economy' is not a simple process and, besides technological innovations, requires negotiation skills. In a circular economy, not all ideas can be applied directly without changes to production technology and the negotiation of legal obstacles. However, the effort seems to be profitable, and not only for financial reasons, but precisely

---

16  Sarah Crean, 'In the Shadow of Real Estate, Linking Designers and Manufacturers', *Progressive Planning* 190 (Winter 2012): 24–26.

because of forced innovations — technological, social and legal. But what is most important here is the anti-individualistic and inclusive perspective, changing not only the work relationship but, in fact, its power to reconstruct the whole society.

As I tried to show, the industrial city (as opposed to the city in which industry is merely present) is a coherent socio-economic project, reinforcing (or even constituting) the city as a subject, understood as a coherent narrative binding residents, institutions, space, activities and everything material in the city. However, the industrial city cannot exist 'by itself'; it must be established and maintained by the outside socio-political and cultural frame, which is transcendent to the materiality of the city. I am not necessarily thinking here in terms of the exterior in the territorial sense (state or supra-state structure), but more about a vision that exceeds the city and gives it a non-immanent purpose.

The industrial city 2.0 is the opposite of the contemporary city, based on the extremely individualistic philosophy of competition. So it is the city based on overcoming selfishness and on the construction of a new, inclusive community (inclusive, however, but not necessarily democratic in the sense that we are used to today). History has not ended, neoliberalism was only a temporary aberration, everything is still ahead of us — we just need to think and act to reach beyond here-and-now. Revolution is always rooted in transcendence.

Chapter 6

# Whose Re-Industrialization? Greening the Pit or Taking Over the Means of Production?

*Malcolm Miles*

In *After London,* published in 1885, naturalist Richard Jeffries describes the city abandoned to nature after an unexplained catastrophe. Within a year everywhere has become overgrown: grasses are overwhelmed by docks and thistles in a pseudo-Darwinian scenario of survival of the strongest. Brambles hide the roads, railway embankments are overgrown by trees. A lake covers much of central England, and London is submerged under a swamp forty miles long into which its buildings have collapsed:

There exhales from this oozy mass so fatal a vapour that no animal can endure it. The black water bears a greenish-brown floating scum, which for ever bubbles up from the putrid mud of the bottom. When the wind collects the miasma ... it becomes visible as a low cloud which hangs over the place. [...] at such times when the vapour is thickest, the very wildfowl leave the reeds, and fly from the poison. [...] It is dead.[1]

---

1   Richard Jeffries, *After London* (1885), cited in J. Carey (ed.), *The Faber Book of Utopias,* 276–78 (London: Faber, 1999), 278.

Fig. 1: Herman Prigann, *Heaven's Ladder,* Gelsenkirchen, Germany, 1997–2000.

Blue flames shoot periodically from the depths of the mire. People say devils live there. The bodies of the dead have dissolved into black mud but their skeletal hands still clutch coins. Jeffries was brought up in rural Wiltshire but moved to Surbiton to earn a living. He became ill, blamed it on putrid black water and a lack of proper drains, and wrote *After London* as his revenge on the city.[2] But the swamp, and the skeletal hands clutching coins, might equally suggest an image of industrial capitalism, the effects of which are described by Friedrich Engels after visiting Manchester in 1844:

> Everything which here arouses horror and indignation is of recent origin, belongs to the *industrial epoch* ... [which] has built up every spot ... to win a covering for the masses whom it has conjured hither from the agricultural districts and from Ireland; the industrial epoch alone enables the owners of these cattle-sheds to rent them for high prices to human beings, to plunder the poverty of the workers, to undermine the health of thousands, to order that they alone, the owners, may grow rich.[3]

The movement to the towns began with the agricultural revolution in the eighteenth century (which was also the beginning of organized labor). As machines replaced workers on farms, so families were driven from their homes and from the land, first to seek work at annual hiring fairs or, if unsuccessful, to wander the roads destitute and malnourished, and later to the towns for other forms of deprivation for low and often seasonal wages in the vile living conditions described by Engels.

The scenario was well known among the educated middle class. Scenes of a lost rural life in the novels of Thomas Hardy, and Alfred Tennyson's vision of a lost chivalric era, are both, in their different (realist and romanticized) ways, displacements. This oblique criticality appealed to the educated, reformist middle class but has become ingrained in English culture to the extent, today, that an idyllic countryside is constructed as a foil to a malodorous and corrupting city. Hence smoke-blackened terraces and smoking chimneys are the epitome of how indus-

---

2   Christopher Woodward, *In Ruins* (London: Vintage, 2002).
3   Friedrich Engels, *The Condition of the Working Class in England in 1844* (London: Allen and Unwin, 1892), cited in James Donald (ed.), *Imagining the Modern City* (London: Athlone, 1999), 36.

trial towns are represented for a mass public, from the novels of Charles Dickens to nineteenth-century prints and the mid-twentieth-century paintings of L.S. Lowry. Since all that occurred, industry itself has been encapsulated in the past as material production has shifted to the global South to be replaced in the North by the immaterial production of culture, media, public relations and financial services.

This move has left new swathes of built and social dereliction. And just as a regression to an imagined rustic life was the displacing reaction of middle-class readers in the late nineteenth century, in the late twentieth century culture has again been central to the displacement of the concept of making (manufacturing) and to the histories of organized labor which occurred in locations such as London's Docklands. Below the shiny towers of late capitalism in Docklands, the only visible reminder of a past of labor is a bronze likeness of three dockers; but this, far from celebrating the labor militancy for which the docks were known, depicts a foreman in a top hat standing over two workers in cloth caps grappling with a load — a social hierarchy maintained. But this time, from the 1980s to the financial services crisis of 2008, culture did not magic a past image but became the future: cool Britannia as the erasure of work and its organization, designer-beer in place of solidarity, and — crucially — a depoliticized culture in place of political contestation..

The standard response to urban deindustrialization, then, is to re-use redundant industrial sites for flagship cultural institutions aimed at attracting tourism and investment (sometimes called the Bilbao effect). In place of soot and disease, the clean post-industrial capitalism of the cultural turn re-appropriates culture's claim in classical thought to universal value, to replace urban blight — a term misleadingly likening a range of linked policy failures to a crop disease — with the new consumer delights of Tate Modern, various Guggenheims, and so forth. Every city seems to seek a place on the globalized culture map by building or converting a new museum of contemporary art.

Meanwhile, urban villages — another nostalgic term adopted now by developers for inner-city gated enclaves — house a cultural class whose lifestyle-consumption feeds malls and art gallery shops in support of the wider project of gentrification. Art, subsumed in entertainment, is an aspirational commodity, and Tate a market leader. Esther Leslie writes,

> Tate is a brand that niche-markets art experience. Its galleries are showrooms. However, this is still art and not just business. The commodity must not show too glossy a face. The reclamation of an industrial space that provides the shell for Tate Modern lends the building a fashionably squatted aspect [...]. At Tate Modern a former industrial site becomes home to the new-style 'accessibility rules' culture industry.[4]

Faced with the excesses of capitalism, George Monbiot advocates a selective return to a pre-industrial economy: re-wilding, introducing wild species such as the lynx in forest areas of Britain, thereby reproducing the nineteenth-century search for a lost rural idyll (which never existed) in a new, post-industrial form. This is not to argue against such re-wilding, which Monbiot sees as applicable only in some places; more to point out that it is a response which distances the proposed solution to urban ills — an over-productive society with excesses of waste as well as wealth divides, and so forth — to the few more or less pre-industrial sites which remain. In fact, in any case, most of those forest and moorland sites are as carefully managed and protected, as reserves, as urban parks are cultivated for leisure. It seems, then, that the industrialized city has become an icon of all that is negative, to be replaced, or mediated by far-away images of, a new kind of wildness. But was industry bad? Industry's benefits were mismanaged and unevenly distributed; still, it produced work and many things which improved our lives. Factories polluted the atmosphere but were where a class seeking to overcome the abuses of capitalism became organized. As the workers of an iron-rolling shop said in Russia in 1917:

---

4   Esther Leslie, 'Tate Modern: A Year of Sweet Success', *Radical Philosophy* 109 (2001): 2–5, at 3.

Fig. 2: Duisburg Nord Landscape Park, Germany.

> If Messrs Capitalists will not pay attention to our demands, then we … demand complete control of all branches of industry by the toiling people. Of you capitalists … we demand that you stop crying about devastation that you yourselves have created. Your cards are on the table. Your game is up.[5]

Something similar might be said now to bankers, commodity speculators and the political elite who have turned the nation-state into an out-sourced provider of governmental services for trans-national capital. What is to be done? Among responses to deindustrialization, apart from cultural colonization, are:

- rehabilitation of ex-industrial sites for community purposes;
- anti-capitalist protest and the evolution of second-hand or non-money economies;
- grass-roots, localized, DIY re-industrialization.

---

5    Quoted in Stephen A. Smith, *The Russian Revolution: A Very Short Introduction* (Oxford: Oxford University Press, 2002), 29.

In the remainder of this chapter I look briefly at each of these (which are not exclusive options).

## Rehabilitation

The Duisburg Nord Landscape Park rehabilitates redundant industrial structures for leisure purposes for the benefit of local communities: abseiling on the exterior and diving in the interior of towers in an old iron works, dog-walking, rambling, simply passing time (since the end of industry produces a time-rich class). Landscaping lends these structures the appearance of the picturesque, but there are also environmental benefits. The nearby Emscher Park, for instance, involved decontaminating the river Emscher and the surrounding land, with new planting and areas left to natural (succession) growth. At Essen, the Zolverein combined mine, coke plant and power station — once the most modern facility in Germany, designed by a Bauhaus architect and opened by Adolf Hitler — houses a design museum, a museum of regional history, changing art exhibitions, a café, and a restaurant in the old turbine hall. This is closer to a cultural project, not least because most of the attractions are indoors, but retains a strong regional emphasis. Again there are large areas of succession growth and the return of bird and insect species. Zolverein does not seem to have caused gentrification, perhaps because the site is on the city's outskirts. But nor have these projects rehabilitated the Ruhr's economy.[6]

Taking a different approach, the German artist Herman Prigann worked in several brownfield sites in the Ruhr and ex-German Democratic Republic (East Germany in colloquial terms), again turning residual industrial sites into post-Romantic ruins but emphasizing the role of succession growth. To take another but subtly different example, at an open-cast brown coal mine near Cotbus, Prigann employed unemployed workers to

---

6    Karl Barndt, 'Memory Traces of an Abandoned Set of Futures: Industrial Ruins and the Post-Industrial Landscapes of Germany', in *Ruins of Modernity*, eds. Julia Hell et al., 270–93 (Durham: Duke University Press, 2010).

build *Die Gelbe Rampe* (1993–94). On the edge of the vast excavation, which is being allowed to flood, Prigann constructed a sloping earthwork topped by a set of concrete slabs as a monument to industry. And by this he meant a monument to celebrate industry and remember it after its passing, not to regret it. The slope is planted with broom which will, in time, spread to cover the ramp. Prigann wrote,

> Nature is neither a thing nor an accumulation of things. It is neither external nor internal, it does not surround us, it is not at our disposition, it cannot be destroyed nor can it be loved.[7]

He saw natural growth as a collaborating agent (an actor in Latour's terms) and intended that it would overtake his work while, at the same time, his interventions would never be entirely obliterated, some trace remaining in drainage patterns or visible in aerial photographs. Prigann was emphatic that industry was not bad, and should not be dismissed; hence his use of discarded industrial material. Although his work is Romantic in a way (and he often cited German Romanticism in conversations), it refuses to be judgmental. I find this hopeful and important. Perhaps a similar attitude could be applied more widely, for instance to international modernism as an intellectual salvage project rather than as a mistake which produced little beyond failed social housing and ring roads, and should be written off.

## Protest

As the welfare state is systematically dismantled and radical arts groups lose their funding, creative energy turns to refusal in a growth of artists' collectives and practices which subvert the art world from within. For instance, Liberate Tate, a London-based group linked to the arts, environment and human rights organization Platform, undertakes projects which could be described

---

7   Hermann Prigann, 'Prologue — Thoughts about Nature', in *Ecological Aesthetics: Art in Environmental Design, Theory and Practice,* eds. Heike Strelow, Hermann Prigann, and Vera David (Basel: Birkhäuser, 2004), 74.

as *re-industrializing* Tate. To remind Tate's audiences of the
link between oil — an industry characterized by human rights
abuses and environmental degradation — and the arts through
sponsorship, Liberate Tate organizes free events at Tate's London branches. In 2010 — the year of the Deepwater Horizon spill
in the Gulf of Mexico — at a party celebrating 20 years of BP's
sponsorship, Toni and Bobbi, posing as guests, allowed an oil-
like substance (molasses) to spill from under their expensive,
flower-patterned skirts and leather handbags. In April 2011, also
at Tate Britain, in *The Human Cost,* a figure rolled on the floor
of Tate Britain covered again in molasses (perhaps reminiscent
of the direct materiality fused with a conceptual critique which
follows from the work of Joseph Beuys). More recently, Liberate Tate carried a wind turbine blade into the Turbine Hall at
Tate Modern to request that it become part of Tate's collection.
The offer was refused despite support from many Tate members.
Liberate Tate describes its work as 'deliberately abject and sometimes foul ... the shadow of an industry the reality of which arts
organizations do not want to see on their doorstep.'[8]

## DIY re-industrialization

At Skinningrove, County Durham (a village written off in the
County Plan in the 1960s), men have built pigeon lofts in what
resembles an informal settlement on the hillside. They cannot
now afford to keep pigeons — big money moved into the bet-
ting — but use the huts as extra living spaces and for black-
economy production such as fish smoking. Skinningrove needs
no art — an art project there failed to engage the community in
the 1990s — because it already has a distinct culture. This suggests that local, tacit knowledge and skills can be used in a grass-
roots re-industrialization outside the regeneration industry and
its ties to either regional bureaucracies or global capital. Such
cases are always local and small-scale, hence easy to dismiss as

---

8   Jo Clarke et al. (eds.), *Not If But When: Culture Beyond Oil* (London: Art
    Not Oil, Liberate Tate and Platform, 2011), 8.

Fig. 3: Pigeon lofts, Skinningrove, County Durham, UK.

irrelevant in the big picture, but they are diverse and numerous as well. At some point, when disillusionment with and anger at top-down improvement schemes reach a peak, grass-roots re-industrialization may produce a renewal of small, local and re-sponsible industries meeting locally identified needs. This may fit in a wider scenario, too: asked about links between Occupy and workers' campaigns, Noam Chomsky said — unexpectedly perhaps — that he saw Occupy as an episode in a class war: a concentration of wealth had led to a concentration of political power and a vicious cycle of anger and frustration.[9] While Andre Gorz argued in the 1980s that the working class had been co-opted to consumerism,[10] Chomsky refers to worker-owned enterprises in de-industrialized zones as another kind of revolution, or taking over the residue of late capitalism by (literally) taking over the management and sites of production. This reminds me that French workers took over and occupied factories in May 1968, following a precedent from the anti-fascist campaigns of the 1930s, not simply to demand better conditions but to demonstrate in practical ways that they could run the factory and organize their own welfare services. In effect, this was an ephemeral taking over of the means of producing society.

Another possibility, also growing, is self-build housing. At Ashley Vale, Bristol, a disused scaffolding yard was used as a self-build site, in an area already an enclave of alternative living with allotments and an urban farm. When the yard closed in 2001 and a developer proposed housing on the site, the land was acquired instead by a local group. Mortgages were arranged for first-time buyers, and plots were sold either for complete self-build or as shells for self-completion. An office block was converted for communal and residential spaces. There are thirty-one houses in various styles using a timber-frame and cladding system like that developed by Walter Segal in the 1970s, and the refurbished office block won the South West Green Energy Award for housing in 2000. A 'Vote Green' sign at the allotment entrance suggests that green living translates into political intention here. Nearby in Stokes Croft, a supermarket was trashed in 2011 after local opposition to its opening. Nearby, a Free Shop denotes a non-money economy. This form of re-industrialization keeps resources in the local economy and creates a state

---

9   Noam Chomsky, *Occupy* (London: Penguin, 2012).
10  André Gorz, *Farewell to the Working Class: An Essay on Post-Industrial Socialism* (London: Pluto, 1982).

within the state in which the values of mutual aid and solidarity are reclaimed amid neoliberal anomie.

## Conclusion

Geographer Erik Swyngedouw identifies an insurgent polis:

> Rethinking [...] the 'Right to the City' as the 'Right to the production of urbanisation'. Henri Lefebvre's clarion call [...] urges us to think of the city as a process of collective codesign and coproduction.[11]

Lefebvre's theory of moments of liberation comes to mind — the idea that sudden, unannounced moments of clarity occur for anyone amid the dulling routines of capitalism — but Lefebvre wrote during the industrial period, when workers' solidarity was a real presence. Today, new kinds of solidarity are needed, and — as the state is as abandoned to capital's excesses as Jeffries' London was abandoned to a swamp — a re-possession of the political and intellectual spaces of the state is necessary, as the protector of the commonwealth (a wealth produced commonly, for common use to meet common needs, rather than the wants manufactured by consumerism): a state of codesign and coproduction applied and adapted on a national scale. This may seem far-fetched, or as Romantic as, say, Tennyson's Arthurian Britain; yet major changes in social values have occurred in modern history. Among them were the abolition of slavery throughout the British Empire in the 1830s, and women's suffrage in Britain in the 1920s. Things do change, all the time. The problem is how to inflect history in the direction of a better world.

---

11  E. Swyngedouw, *Designing the Post-Political City and the Insurgent Polis* (London: Bedford Press, 2011), 53.

# Chapter 7

# Crowdsourced Urbanism? The Maker Revolution and the Creative City 2.0

*Doreen Jakob*

Cutting the ribbon at the opening of the new Shapeway factory, New York City Mayor Michael Bloomberg proclaims that the 3-D printing company will form 'a critical bridge between the tech and manufacturing centers [... and] help us bring the city's industrial sector directly into the twenty-first century'.[1] He announces: 'this is the future of our city'.[2] According to Anderson, today's maker movement is the newest, third industrial revolution.[3] Rifkin argues that 'like every other economic revolution that preceded it, The Third Industrial [Revolution] will recast many of our assumptions about how the world works'.[4] Thus what future and what city does the maker movement create? This book questions whether urban re-industrialization can be

---

1   Kelly Faircloth, 'At a Ribbon-Cutting for Shapeways' "Factory of the Future"', *The Observer,* October 18, 2012, http://observer.com/2012/10/shapeways-grand-opening-factory-long-island-city-michael-bloomberg-mayor-3d-printing/.

2   Ibid.

3   Chris Anderson, *Makers: The New Industrial Revolution* (New York: Crown Business, 2012).

4   Jeremy Rifkin, *The Third Industrial Revolution: How Lateral Power Is Transforming Energy, the Economy, and the World* (New York: Palgrave Macmillan, 2011), 189.

imagined as a progressive socio-political and economical project leading to an inclusive and democratic society based on cooperation and symbiosis. Many of the conference's presentations offered examples of how to envision urban re-industrialization. In this short chapter, however, I argue that urban re-industrialization as part of a third industrial revolution is not a distant futuristic concept but a reality in the making. Driven by the maker movement, green energy, crowdsourcing and crowd-funding, the third industrial revolution comes along dressed in the flowing robes of collaboration, participation, democratized manufacturing and 'distributed capitalism'.[5] It iterates the promises of the 'Creative City'.[6] Yet unlike its predecessor, it show-cases tangible, three-dimensional products instead of intangible soft location factors, crowd financing instead of public-private-partnerships.[7] The Creative City 2.0 features applicability and dispersion. However, its practical and distributive appeal simultaneously allows for additional and more effective ways to hide its entrepreneurial and non-democratic nature. The Creative City characterizes a form and process of urbanization in which creativity stands at the forefront.[8] However, more commonly it is seen as a set of policy and planning mechanisms that, once applied, result in a Creative City. According to Landry, the Creative City 'describes a new method of strategic urban planning and examines how people can think, plan and act creatively in the city. It explores how we can make our cities more livable and vital by harnessing people's imagination and talent'.[9] Landry and Bianchini[10] advocate for a more holistic understanding of crea-

---

5    Jeremy Rifkin, 'The Third Industrial Revolution: How the Internet, Green Electricity, and 3-D Printing are Ushering in a Sustainable Era of Distributed Capitalism', *World Financial Review*, 1 (2012): 4052–57.

6    Charles Landry, *The Creative City: A Toolkit for Urban Innovators* (London: Comedia, 2008).

7    Doreen Jakob, 'Constructing the Creative Neighborhood: Hopes and Limitations of Creative City Policies in Berlin', *City, Culture and Society* 1 (2010): 193–98.

8    Ibid.

9    Landry, *The Creative City*, xii.

10    C. Landry and F. Bianchini, *The Creative City* (London: Demos, 1995).

tivity that also includes social and political reform in addition to artistic and technological innovation. In many ways, their ideas answer positively to the conference organizers' question of imagining urban re-industrialization 'beyond the current model of a neoliberal city'. In practice, however, the real 'creativity' of the Creative City model tends to be its ability to reframe and repackage an entrepreneurial model of urban governance and development geared towards attracting highly mobile capital and professional elites with environments to live and work in, as well as to consume and invest in, that are lively yet safe, diverse yet controlled, artistic yet profit-driven. While much of the past Creative City and Creative Class[11] debates centered on individualized lifestyles, now comes a second generation of Creative City-making policies that focuses on shared production: the Creative City 2.0. Formerly lacking democratic participation, the Creative City 2.0 features 'democracy' and 'participation' in the form of crowdsourced and crowdfunded urbanism. Often called 'Kickstarter urbanism',[12] in reference to one of the most prominent crowdfunding companies, Kickstarter, crowdfunding provides an effective appearance of collaborative decision-making. Overall, there are more than 450 crowdfunding platforms worldwide that supported over 100,000 projects in 2012.[13] Kickstarter was founded in 2009 in New York City and soon became the 'world's largest funding platform for creative projects' with more than 4.4 million people having funded over 44,000 creative projects with more than US$685 million. The company provides an online fundraising platform that simultaneously functions as a marketing as well as opinion-polling tool. It is often praised by members of the maker community as a 'game

---

11  Richard Florida, *The Rise of the Creative Class: And How It's Transforming Work, Leisure, Community and Everyday Life* (New York: Perseus Book Group, 2002).

12  A. Lange, 'Against Kickstarter Urbanism', *The Design Observer Group,* May 2, 2012, http://designobserver. com/feature/against-kickstarter-urbanism/34008/.

13  Brian Boyer and Dan Hill, *Brickstarter* (Helsinki: Sitra, 2013), http://www.brickstarter.org/Brickstarter.pdf.

changer' [14] for the development of prototypes and first manu-facturing runs of design products. Yet, the Kickstarter versus National Endowment for the Arts (NEA)[15] debate illustrates[16] the company's success is not without perils and criticism. As I have pointed out elsewhere, arts and cultural funding in the United States is much more diverse and dispersed, and characterized by much lesser relative government support compared to many European countries.[17] Hence, the possibility of Kickstarter funding being equal to or surpassing the NEA not only shows the strength of the former but also the weakness of the latter. The main issue, however, is not numbers but the idea that companies like Kickstarter represent a 'people's N.E.A.'[18]

Crowdfunding as currently practiced is not democratic. It creates an illusion of democracy. Kickstarter staff review all submitted projects favoring 'creators who think through the re-wards for backers, get the word out and engage an audience. In other words, the process doesn't shape the aesthetic. It is the aesthetic'[19]. Curatorial emphasis is not on the final product but on how well its creators will market and sell their fundraising campaign.

---

14  Anderson, *Makers*.

15  The NEA is the US government's federal arts and cultural funding body.

16  E.g., Ian Moss, "Art and Democracy: The NEA, Kickstarter, and Creativity in America," *Createquity*, April 9, 2012, http://createquity.com/2012/04/art-and-democracy-the-nea-kickstarter-and-creativity-in-america.html.  See also Carl Franzen, 'NEA Weighs In On Kickstarter Funding Debate', *Talking Points Memo*, February 27, 2012, http://talkingpointsmemo.com/idealab/nea-weighs-in-on-kickstarter-funding-debate.

17  Doreen Jakob, *Beyond Creative Production Networks: The Development of Intra-Metropolitan Creative Industries Clusters in Berlin and New York City* (Berlin: Rhombos, 2009); D. Jakob, '"To Have and to Need": Reorganizing Cultural Policy as Panacea for Berlin's Urban and Economic Woes', in *The Politics of Urban Cultural Policy: Global Perspectives*, eds. C. Grodach and D. Silvereds, 110–21 (New York: Routledge, 2013).

18  Rob Walker, 'The Trivialities and Transcendence of Kickstarter', *The New York Times Magazine*, August 5, 2011, http://www.nytimes.com/2011/08/07/magazine/the-trivialities-and-transcendence-of-kickstarter.html.

19  Ibid.

This is most problematic for urban and neighborhood development projects. As Lange writes, with Kickstarter urban development loses out to industrial design:

> You wouldn't Kickstart a replacement bus line for Brooklyn, but you might Kickstart an app to tell you when the bus on another, less convenient line might come. You can't Kickstart affordable housing, but the really cool tent for the discussion thereof. [...] [W]orthy goals have to be dressed up in complex geometries for Kickstarter. [...] [However, t]he park is going to require a lot more doing than $5 and 'Great idea!'[20]

Many urban development projects are not only more expensive than the production of a music album or a new video game; they also require a much larger timeframe from the initial idea to completion. They are place-specific and fixed, and hence much more dependent on local support and less able to generate the broad, worldwide support needed for large capital projects. Moreover, successfully securing funding does not automatically mean that projects will pass local zoning regulations and permits. Once a project is approved and on-site development starts, 'what happens when the project runs over budget, as many capital projects do? Are donors obligated to chip in for overages?'[21] Once it is completed, 'who is responsible for it? Who bears responsibility in 60 years? Whereas consumer products can be recycled or discarded, it's not as simple to do the same with pieces of the city'.[22]

Companies like Kickstarter do not own the final products that are fundraised for on their websites, nor do the funders. Kickstarter collects a 5% fee on successfully funded projects. Supporters receive numerous gifts depending on how much money they pledge. Now Fundrise, a new urban development

---

20 Lange, 'Against Kickstarter Urbanism'.
21 Brian Boyer, 'Pools are Expensive (Thoughts about the Long Tail and Crowdfunding)', *Brickstarter*, March 26, 2012, http://brickstarter.org/pools-are-expensive-thoughts-about-the-long-tail-and-crowdfunding/.
22 Boyer and Hill, *Brickstarter*, 27.

company, is setting an example to change that system so that the funding crowds can become real estate investors and collect returns. Aiming to reform urban financing, Fundrise's founders believe they have found a way that is 'really potentially a radical transformation of urban planning, of development, of investment, of local government'.[23] The company utilizes Regulation A of the US Securities and Exchange Commission that permits small offerings to unaccredited investors, as well as the April 2012 Jumpstart Our Business Startups (JOBS) Act that eases various securities regulations. Fundrise has received much attention within the past few months, including a presentation in front of the US House subcommittee on finance innovation in June 2013, and is hailed by supporters as a way to democratize finance and 'remak[e] the very places where we live'.[24]

Yet the praise for democratization is treacherous. Surely, companies like Kickstarter and Fundrise enable project financing that moves beyond the wealthy patron and foreign real estate investor, respectively. They provide opportunities for more people to finance interesting projects. But more is not everybody, equally, democratically. Kickstarter's focus on selling ideas and designing enticing marketing campaigns makes humble yet realizable neighborhood development projects bid—and often lose—against pretentious yet less attainable ideas.[25] Fundrise's projects are not about investing in basic services in disadvan-

---

23  B. Miller, quoted in E. Badger, 'The Real Estate Deal That Could Change the Future of Everything', *CityLab*, November 19, 2012, http://www.citylab.com/work/2012/11/real-estate-deal-could-change-future-everything/3897/.

24  Ibid.

25  For instance, Lange provides examples of two urban development projects in the very same neighborhood: the LowLine, a 1.5 acre abandoned trolley terminal to be turned into an underground park, and the effort to fund a new Ping-Pong table for an existing (aboveground) neighborhood park. The first raised US$155,000, while the latter failed to secure the US$4,200 needed. Yet, the Ping-Pong table could have been set up and useable in relatively short time; the LowLine Kickstarter financed none but a test of the skylights that would filter the daylight underground. 'The consumable dream was years and bureaucracies away': Lange, 'Against Kickstarter Urbanism'.

taged neighborhoods, and the renderings and promotion videos of their H Street, Washington, DC projects feature white, young professionals and advertise the street's 'thriving social scene'.[26] Overall, the current most prominent crowdfunding models operate on a form of participation that is nothing more than diffused monetary investments.

The third industrial revolution is, according to Rifkin, characterized by democratized manufacturing and distributed capitalism.[27] It is a revolution driven by urbanized making.[28] Yet, urban re-industrialization, unlike its predecessor, cannot have a foundation of heavy machinery and gigantic factories employing hundreds of workers making thousands of products. Instead, technologies like 3D printing could theoretically enable everybody to host their very own 'factory' on their bedside table and produce 'one of a kind' creations. Beyond the individual, the maker revolution could feature crowdsourcing and crowdfunding. Yet, this type of play with 'distributed capitalism'[29] never questions the principles of capitalism. Crowdfunded urban development projects feature a further spectacularization[30] and monetization of neighborhood development. Contemporary urban re-industrialization in this form is neither a progressive socio-political and economical project, nor does it lead to an inclusive and democratic society based on cooperation and symbiosis. The Creative City 2.0 as envisaged in this construct is a profit-generating machine dressed up in the noble concepts of democracy and participation.

---

26  See https://fundrise.com/investments.

27  Rifkin, 'The Third Industrial Revolution'.

28  Anderson, *Makers*.

29  Rifkin, 'The Third Industrial Revolution'.

30  Doreen Jakob, 'The Eventification of Place: Urban Development and Experience Consumption in Berlin and New York City', *European Urban and Regional Studies* 20, no. 4 (2013): 447–59.

Chapter 8

# Brave New World?!

*Tatjana Schneider*

This chapter takes its title from Aldous Huxley's famous novel of the same name. Set in the very distant future of the year 2540, the novel outlines a world in which every being's rank in society is predetermined at embryo-stage. Once in the world, ranks and happiness within one's rank are then managed by a drug with the name of *soma*. Highly influential on many levels, the novel raises interesting philosophical questions around concepts such as manipulation, design, free will, and liberty and (pre-)determination amongst others. Given, for example, that the individuals in Huxley's novel have been engineered before birth, are they truly responsible for their actions or are they merely the tools of their designers at the *Hatchery and Conditioning Centre?* And does the manufacturing process create individuals who are, as the American philosopher Gary Watson declares, 'incapable of effectively envisaging or seeing the significance of certain alternatives, of reflecting on [themselves] and on the origins of [their] motivations'?[1]

By referring to Huxley's novel and some of the philosophical questions around freedom to act or lack thereof, this chapter explores two interrelated topics. On the one hand, I argue that despite current society not being engineered in the same way

---

1   G. Watson, quoted in Kadri Vihvelin, 'Arguments for Incompatibilism', *Stanford Encyclopedia of Philosophy* (Spring 2011 Edition), ed. Edward N. Zalta, http://plato.stanford.edu/entries/incompatibilism-arguments/.

as Huxley's society, when it comes to the production of space it seems we are unable to see beyond the current systems and practices, in particular capitalism. Actions executed with the best and most radical of intentions are often used and counter-appropriated to reinforce the current state of affairs. This is where the exclamation mark after the title comes from. On the other hand, I also believe that brave and therefore bold actions are necessary to envisage and also produce alternate futures. The question mark in the title points, therefore, both to the perceived and real probabilities of a non-capitalist production of space and its consequences.

The discussion in this chapter loosely follows the broad questions that were posed by the 'Re-industrialisation and Progressive Urbanism' conference (held at Plymouth University in June 2013) that was the force behind this book. It covers the possibilities of re-industrialization and much more, but before continuing any further I would like to clarify those key questions. In the call for papers, Dr. Krzysztof Nawratek, invited responses to questions about the possibility of imagining re-industrialization as a 'progressive socio-political and economical project, aiming to create an inclusive and democratic society based on cooperation and symbiosis that goes way beyond the current model of a neoliberal city'.[2]

My immediate response, from my hopeful half, gave a resounding 'Yes!' Yes, of course, re-industrialization could be imagined as a progressive project — and, even better, there really is no need for imagining this. Abundant examples of this exist already — not necessarily related to the issue of re-industrialization, but certainly within the wider spectrum of spatial productions. There are, my hopeful half insists, plenty of small and large projects that contribute to the democratic and social production of space and do indeed challenge increasingly commodified and unjust developments.

---

2    Krzysztof Nawratek, 'Re-industrialisation and Progressive Urbanism' conference, School of Architecture, Design and Environment, Plymouth University, June 13, 2013. The call for papers was issued on February 25, 2013.

But then, of course, there is also my pessimistic and doubtful half, which quickly interjects with: 'Well, I'm not so sure about your optimism — it actually does look rather grim at the moment'. We only need to look at the destruction of the welfare state in the UK and many other European countries, for example, which happens within the general promise and premise of progress, greater participation and inclusion on a local level. Worst of all, much of this discourse and debate around this supposedly progressive notion of planning happens under the auspices of, and using the vocabulary of, the Left — and, even worse, without too much resistance from the Left, really. At the same time there is also, and I'm guilty of this too, a retreat into what you could call 'the small-scale stuff'. A retreat, you could say, into these little niches that make us believe that the world can be a better place.

As a citizen I am keen to believe, but maybe I am only led or even conditioned to believe, that the world would indeed be a better place if only more of us would do the little things that matter. Things such as shop locally, recycle, engage in the local transition town movement, grow our own vegetables, join the Green Party and Ecotricity, move my current account to the Co-operative Bank and my savings account to Triodos, and also, of course, join the local cohousing group. And so the list goes.

By switching accounts and changing my shopping habits, I tell myself, I'm not only acting on a hunch. There is real evidence to justify these actions. I only need to look again at Nabeel Hamdi's book *Small Change* in which he argues that 'intelligent practice builds on the collective wisdom of people and organizations on the ground — those who think locally and act locally — which is then rationalized in ways that make a difference globally'.[3] Hamdi goes on: 'Good development practice facilitates emergence; it builds on what we've got and with it goes to scale'.[4] And more: 'in order to do something big — to think

---

3    Nabeel Hamdi, *Small Change: About the Art of Practice and the Limits of Planning in Cities* (London: Earthscan, 2004), xviii.

4    Ibid.

globally and act globally — one starts with something small, and one starts where it counts.[5]

'Phew!' my hopeful half goes again. Thinking and acting locally is precisely what I do. If Hamdi emphasizes the importance, indeed the necessity, of the local — of each and every one of us doing what he or she can — not all can be lost.

But then, of course, my doubtful half is quick to point out that Hamdi is not only talking about the local on its own, by itself. In fact, he explicitly addresses the elephant in the room — namely the necessity of scaling up, or more concretely, the interdependence of the small and the large. Further, he talks about scaling up not just for the sake of scaling up, but scaling up as a means to induce wider, arguably social, changes.

Let's pick this up: social change. Social change is something that is being talked and written about a lot. 'Small change' (which is here used as equivalent to 'local change'), it is often argued, leads to social change. Consequently, lots of instances of small change put together will eventually, but inevitably, change the way we produce, consume, exchange and also distribute. In effect, this powerful force of combined small changes will force the induction of much bigger and systemic change.

The political economist Greg Sharzer is probably one of the most fervent opponents of this way of thinking. He writes: 'The localist form of citizenship may empower us, but it cannot confront capitalism. Against a global network of power must emerge globalised forms of struggle.'[6] Sharzer doesn't have any sympathies for localism and localists. In his book *No Local: Why Small-Scale Alternatives Won't Change the World,* Sharzer argues that localists would not choose to be localists if they had, I quote, 'a greater understanding of how capitalism works'.[7]

So, how does capitalism work?

---

5   Ibid., xiv.

6   Greg Sharzer, 'Local Resistance to Global Austerity: It Will Never Work', *openDemocracy*, January 3, 2013, http://www.opendemocracy.net/ourking-dom/greg-sharzer/local-resistance-to-global-austerity-it-will-never-work.

7   Greg Sharzer, *No Local: Why Small-Scale Alternatives Won't Change The World* (Winchester: Zero Books, 2012), 2.

Very simply put, capitalism is about the exploitation of wage labour and the reduction of social relations to commodity exchange or a series of commodity exchanges. Capitalist principles permeate our socio-economic system — on the large and the small scale. But, if we accept that the basic premise of capitalism is exploitation, it follows that it can never be fair. And neither can it be inclusive. Capitalism is effectively undemocratic. As such, it seems quite unsuited — as a socio-economic model — to drive any form of development.

Obviously, it is easy to dismiss this critique of capitalism. I almost understand this possible dismissal. After all, what I am calling for — or at least what my hopeful half is wishing, but also calling for — is an overthrow of capitalism. And that, it is easily argued, is absolutely unrealistic; it is simply not going to happen. My hopeful half disagrees with this, but I also recognize that a focus on individualized responses to and reactions against capitalism cannot provide a viable alternative to it. What is needed is a global, yet localized perspective and response to this problem. A response that is not set within the capitalistic framework because — as I said before — it is inherently unjust. What is needed instead is a new framework that doesn't exploit but allows or affords equitable development. But, what might this look like?

In recent years — and in particular since the beginning of the most recent economic crisis — architecture and design professionals have become quite vocal about the capability of design to make a difference to the world. Many publications, exhibitions and events are investigating the social potential of architecture or architecture's social production. For many, the mere usage of the term 'social' in relation to architecture or spatial production seems to conjure up a panacea for a profession whose practice, as the lawyer and urban planner Peter Marcuse argues, 'has become a training ground for cutting-edge design, cutting-edge not in a social sense or in a human sense, but in a sense of a marketing device that will appeal to clients, that will appeal to those with the money to hire architects'.[8] But what is 'cutting-edge' social design? Does Marcuse refer to the multitude of participatory programs to develop a local school, collaborative processes that go into the production of an urban garden with community space or the sweat equity that goes into the building of a new housing scheme?

It is easy to see the real difference these projects make and therefore become submerged in this turn towards, and the admiration of, so-called 'social architecture'. Social architecture comes with so much promise, so much hope about design's potential to, after all, truly contribute to society. It focuses and also cherishes approaches that, in the words of the feminist Donna Haraway, actively allow for 'partial, locatable, critical knowledges'[9] and at the same time counter what has been portrayed by Mike Davis as an 'unprecedented abyss of economic and social turmoil that confounds our previous perceptions of historical risk'.[10]

However, we ought not to lose sight of the bigger picture. Yes, 'social architecture' is popular because we can see the real difference these projects make on a micro-level. But if we are really honest, most 'social architectures' and so-called 'responsible' actions leave the centre, the predominant socio-economic and cultural system, unscathed. Doing good but incredibly isolated things, leads to the reproduction of smaller, but fundamentally still capitalist, versions of the same thing — and therefore fails to engage with such fundamental issues like socio-economic inequality. And if you believe in global justice, like my hopeful half does, spatial development needs to confront capitalism through organized global socio-spatial movements which are framed

---

8   P. Marcuse, 'What Has to Be Done — The Potentials and Failures of Planning: History, Theory, and Actuality. Lessons from New York', *AnArchitektur* 14 (March 2005): 36–40.

9   Donna Haraway, 'Situated Knowledges: The Science Question in Feminism and the Privilege of Partial Perspective', *Feminist Studies* 14 (1988): 575–99, at 584.

10  Mike Davis, 'US Elections — the New Deal?', *Socialist Review* 330 (November 2008), http://www.socialist review.org.uk/article.php?articlenumber=10589.

by local readings and understandings of culture, practice and space. So, let's stop the glorification of 'social architecture', and begin to construct, as well as enact, global narratives that will allow the formation of a wider alliance concerned with the just production of space. To be very clear, I'm not talking about the implementation of a supposedly 'greener' or 'softer' option of capitalism, but social forms of production that are not only collectively produced but also socially appropriated.

There is no need to start from scratch. The 1980s squatting movement in West Berlin highlights the powerful force of collective action, collective production and social appropriation that led to a change in spatial politics. There also the various Latin American Residential Organisations, of which some help to organize and implement the actual construction and management of housing and others concentrate on training and political reform. And there are many more.

My doubtful half begins to tell me off again for being optimistic. However, and not only because I want to end with a hopeful note, the two examples mentioned — each on their own scale and with their obvious limitations — begin to draw attention to the real possibilities of a different economy and also to how social production can lead to processes and products that are transformative on many levels.

Chapter 9

# The Political Agency of Geography and the Shrinking City

*Jeffrey T. Kruth*

Traveling down Chester Road from downtown Cleveland, a beacon of architectural modernity can be seen reflecting light off the Norman Foster-designed medical campus, signaling that one has reached an urbanism vastly different from the one just traversed. An institutional heterotopia of sorts, the extensive campus stands in as a symbol for a coherent urban language amid a decaying landscape of vacant parcels and foreclosed homes. The region's largest employer and primary economic driver since the 1980s, the Cleveland Clinic's economic impact is roughly $12.6 billion, and by extension, its employees contribute $5.9 billion to the Ohio economy.[1] World renowned for its healthcare and research contributions, the Clinic and nearby institutions of the 'med-ed' complex — University Hospitals and Case Western Reserve University — provide an economic stability in a city that has struggled to prove itself as resilient for more than a generation.

In the surrounding neighborhoods of the University Circle area, there is a 25% unemployment rate and the city as a whole claims a whopping 33% poverty rate, or approximately 118,000

---

1   Cleveland Clinic, *Cleveland Clinic: A Vital Force in Ohio's Economy* (2014), https://my.clevelandclinic.org/ccf/media/Files/About-Cleveland-Clinic/economic-impact-report/economic-impact-report-2015-Ohio.pdf?la=en

of its 396,000 residents. The population in the city proper has dropped by more than half in recent decades. Peaking at 900,000 residents in the 1950s, the onslaught of de-industrialization in the Midwestern United States leaves Cleveland standing as one of several poster children cities of the enigmatic 'Rust Belt'. Additionally, the onset of the financial crisis in the mid-2000s caused housing prices to drop by roughly 30%.[2] Speculative investors and poor appraisal practices have only added to the detrimental effects of a weak housing market. Approximately 20,000 vacant lots dot the landscape throughout the city, a testament to the city's continual decline. Cheap land and taxes (approximately 36% of vacant land in Cleveland is tax-abated), push the boundary of development further into more affluent suburbs, leaving the inner city devoid of critical infrastructure and a solid economic tax base. The Clinic liberally expands to the suburbs, creating services in wealthier ones where many of their patients reside, furthering competition between the City of Cleveland and other municipalities for the externality benefits of a Clinic development.

The anchor institutions of the 'med-ed' complex benefit from tax exempt status as non-profit organizations, while its spatial clout recently expanded through the creation of a special development district — labeled the 'Health-Tech Corridor' — along a 4.5-mile stretch between downtown and the University Circle area.[3] This area prioritizes development for medical technology startups as well as the anchor institutions themselves. As the largest holder of vacant, tax-abated land in the city, the Clinic also takes advantage of city programs such as the Vacant Properties Initiative (VPI), which grants loans for the development of vacant land.[4] A mere 8% of the city's revenue comes from property taxes, while 55% of it comes from income taxes, which is an

2    A. Friedhoff and S. Kulkarni, 'Metro Monitor — March 2013,' The Brookings Institution, last modified March 20, 2015.

3    'Cleveland Health-Tech Corridor', http://www.healthtechcorridor.com/.

4    City of Cleveland Department of Economic Development, *Report to Council 2010*, http://www.cdfa.net/cdfa/cdfaweb.nsf/ordredirect. html?open&id=clev2010report.html.

inverted formula compared to many American cities, starving Cleveland of a solid tax base.[5] Even in comparable Rust Belt cities like nearby Pittsburgh, Pennsylvania, property taxes account for nearly double the income tax base.[6]

These spatial and policy tactics are indicative not only of political mismanagement at the local level, but also a neoliberal spatial ideology. In an age where financial capital is hardly dependent on geography or even on workers, institutional campuses have become a normative extension of a particular strand of neoliberal spatial ideology. In order to remain competitive at a global level, institutions in the 'med-ed' model must embark on a sort of geographic imperialism in order to capitalize on their suburban as well as their international markets.[7] This model of the local gone global ensures that the Clinic remains competitive at the international level. It is no longer just necessary to provide ground-breaking work in research or technology, it is also necessary to embark on a geographic campaign, erecting new campuses across the globe as a new form of imperialism. In this way, the Clinic and other anchor institutions fit into Michael Hardt and Antonio Negri's concept of *Empire,* which puts forth the theory of a new hegemonic global geopolitical order.

As late capitalism expands into what Hardt and Negri refer to as a bio-political age (taking from Michel Foucault and others), the tools for restructuring a critical class-based project exist within capitalism's current logic. In the bio-political mode of production, work expands beyond the factory walls into daily and social life. Social relations, incessant innovation, knowledge power and privatization of the commons are central aspects in this mode of production. The city itself is central to bio-politi-

---

5   City of Cleveland, *City of Cleveland 2012 Budget Book* (2012), 57. http://webapp.cleveland-oh.gov/aspnet/docs/get.aspx?id=988&file=2012Budget.pdf

6   Pittsburgh City Council, *City of Pittsburgh Pennsylvania Budget 2011* (2011), http://www.city.pittsburgh.pa.us/main/assets/budget/2011/2011-Operating-Capital-Budget.pdf.

7   McClain Clutter, 'Cleveland: Medi-Plex City', in *Formerly Urban: Projecting Rust Belt Futures,* ed. J. Czerniak, 50–69 (New York: Princeton Architectural Press, 2013).

cal production, and to some extent explains the movement of the masses of educated and wealthy classes back to cities in the United States. Creating a 'playground' for social production in gentrified neighborhoods allows for the constant re-invention of fads, ideas, technology and marketing strategies, while constant social production further enables a self-disciplining society and what Sharon Zukin calls 'pacification by cappuccino'.

The med-ed complex is one type of this system in action. In the Fordist mode of production, the city was developed for maximum infrastructural and economic efficiency (moving from 'the City Beautiful' to 'the City Practical'), putting the constant process of urbanization at the forefront of a development strategy. As industrial production fades into a knowledge and financially-based speculative economy, Marx's formulation of the struggle between immobile property (such as land) and moveable property such as material commodities resurfaces as a potential point of political organization.[8] As Hardt points out, 'Property is becoming a fetter on the capitalist mode of production [...] the more the common is corralled as property, the more its productivity is reduced; and yet expansion of the common undermines the relations of property in a fundamental and general way'.[9] Following the Hardt and Negri line, capitalist production is returning to rent-based speculation and market dominance, as opposed to profitability based on the traditional means of production. That is, corporations and institutions are not necessarily seeking to enhance profitability by trimming workers' wages, improving production time, or making supply chain management more efficient. Rather, prices reflect *perceived* market value. And when a few institutions control a large share of a particular market, say vacant land, they can artificially control prices, which can prolong economic distress. This geographic campaign is, in a sense, central to the long-term stability of the anchor institutions to build institutional capacity at

---

8   Michael Hardt, 'The Common in Communism', in *The Idea of Communism*, eds. C. Douzinas and S. Žižek, 131–44 (London: Verso, 2010), 133–36.
9   Ibid., 136.

a local and global scale. Not only does cheap land ensure that more resources can be devoted to the 'bottom line', it enables concentrated large-scale development, typically for the 'creative class', evidenced by the recent Uptown development by Stanley Saitowitz near the anchor institutions. In short, it is in the interest of the anchor institutions to keep land prices low to ensure that development occurs as they see fit — a gross large-scale privatization of spatial production, enabled by city policy.

Just a short ride from both downtown and the University Circle area, a large green house containing Green City Growers occupies a 4.4-acre (1.78-ha) site, holding the country's largest urban hydroponic farm. Initiated in 2007, Green City Growers is one of three worker-owned cooperatives in the city called Evergreen Cooperatives. Based on the highly successful Mondragon model from the Basque region of Spain, the Evergreen model offers the 'one worker, one vote' principle, with every employee being a worker-owner of the cooperative. A certain percentage of each worker's earnings are placed into an internal account, making $65,000 available as a personal capital account at the end of eight years. The Evergreen Cooperatives are also putting in place a formal, centralized financing agency to help finance other cooperatives' development.[10] Although a for-profit enterprise, the cooperatives are worker-owned, sustainably focused and with the highest-paid employee's salary capped, typically at a 3:1 ratio.

Three primary businesses have been started by the Evergreen Cooperatives and have come online since 2009, including the Green City Growers who grow hydroponic produce in the greenhouse, the Ohio Cooperative Solar, which installs photovoltaic panels on buildings and Evergreen Laundry, which is a sustainable laundry facility. The goal is to establish ten cooperatives over the next five years, eventually employing 500 people in living-wage jobs. Far from a grassroots, bottom-up approach,

---

10 Capital Institute, *Field Guide to Investing in a Resilient Economy: Evergreen Cooperatives Field Study* (2012), 6, http://fieldguide.capitalinstitute.org/uploads/1/3/9/6/13963161/_fs2-evergreen_8pg.pdf.

the Mondragon model exercised by the Evergreen Cooperatives takes the city's anchor institutions as its starting point, both for funding and as their client base of their services. The Evergreen Laundry Cooperative serves both the Clinic and University Hospitals, cleaning their linens, while the largest client for Ohio Cooperative Solar has been the Cleveland Clinic's expanding complexes.

The Evergreen Land Trust (coupled with the Evergreen Co-operative Development Fund) was established to work with banks and local authorities to establish new sites for the development of future Evergreen ventures. Assets are primarily directed towards commercial development, structured in a way such that if the Evergreen business were ever to collapse, the Evergreen Land Trust would have the residual right to step in and buy back the building, reducing some of the risk associated with a new business.[11] Discussions are currently underway to address issues like affordable housing development, which may carry fewer risks than commercial development and new business startups. Ohio Cooperative Solar is also considering entering the demolition business for vacant homes in possession of the land bank to account for times of slow business, providing workers with further skill sets.

If the Evergreen Cooperatives were to embark on this type of development venture, then it is here that a potentially counter-hegemonic political and spatial project resides. As the production of space and the city become ever more important in a bio-political age, an inversion of the single-lot, single-owner model may provide context for an alternative form of development — particularly after the subprime foreclosure crisis. In a shrinking city with an oversupply of housing stock and vacant land (the Cleveland Land Bank controls approximately 7,500 of the 20,000 vacant lots city-wide), an alternative regional narrative could be developed through land ownership, applying the Evergreen cooperative model of ownership to land at a large

---

11   Ibid., 18.

scale, expanding political agency to local and perhaps regional politics.

With this, there is an inherently embedded concern with active and productive uses of land, beyond speculative land holding or the more profitable concentration of development of cheap housing or shopping malls. Applying the 'buy-in' model of Mondragon, space can be re-conceived as something which even persons of low and moderate income may buy into. Over time, this creates community wealth, a more stable economic landscape, and communal benefits. As opposed to singular vacant lots, which cause devastating effects on otherwise stable neighborhoods, risk is dispersed amongst multiple owners over multiple lots. The same 'one person-one vote' may likewise apply to land deals, under a larger umbrella of the Evergreen constituency. The same principles of 'people over profit' could also apply, offering an ideological understanding of land as something beyond simply a monetized object. Through cooperative ownership under the umbrella of the Evergreen Cooperatives, a new production of 'the commons' results — offering new forms of knowledge, worker/owner solidarity, an alternative development model and a new class of owners who were formerly excluded.[12]

With an already aggressive demolition schedule, the city may cede some of this work to a newly formed Evergreen business. Whereas building in the single-lot, single-owner model made economic sense for financiers and developers, it lacked a spatial, infrastructural or ecological logic. Through a strategic demolition schedule and creating property interdependence, building destruction may become a profitable venture for the Evergreen cooperatives. That is to say, through strategic planning in cooperation with the city, multiple lots may be assembled for ownership by an Evergreen-like cooperative, which in turn densifies the sites and then creates more tax revenue for the city. The cooperative owners of the densified sites could be tied remotely

---

12  Michael Hardt and Antonio Negri, *Commonwealth* (Cambridge: The Belknap Press of Harvard University Press, 2009), 249–60.

to other hedge spaces that are seeking to be assembled.[13] This creates interest for them through a diversified portfolio and provides incentives for nearby owners to either join the co-op or sell, as market prices stabilize.

While organizing along traditional progressive lines is important, it is also about finding a political and economic alternative to current capitalist practices through a geographic and spatial production agenda. As David Harvey and others have suggested, class struggle is no longer tied to just the workplace but to almost all facets of life, and we must organize the city along geographic lines. The factory is no longer the sole site of capitalist production — it is now the city and everyday urban life. As public life appears to dissolve in a bio-political age, a shared cooperative development strategy would necessarily create political stakeholders amongst the classes of those typically excluded from the public process.[14] Micro-parcelization strategies in India, increased worker cooperatives of the informal economy in the *favelas* of Brazil and public control over infrastructural and natural resources in Bolivia are beginning to create new strategies for organization across the globe. The shrinking cities of the West must likewise embrace the geographic potential for political organization in the metropolis.

Beyond the simple suggestion of housing cooperatives or institutional land banking, such an alternative is about the restructuring of a progressive political project on two levels: first, by placing at the forefront the idea of the commons in a bio-political era and second, by appropriating agency to neighborhoods through social ownership and organizing around the idea of geography to perpetuate the idea of the 'right to the city'. This is especially important given the current development paradigms which solve the problems of the common through traditional neoliberal spatial fixes such as gentrification, privately owned

---

13  Keller Easterling, 'Take-Away', in *Perspecta 45: Agency,* eds. H. Evans et al., 157–60 (Cambridge: MIT Press, 2012).

14  David Harvey, *Rebel Cities: From the Right to the City to the Urban Revolution* (London: Verso, 2012), 115–19.

public space, large scale development for private interests and the control of vacant land by institutions. The task of architects, urbanists and progressive policy makers in the coming years will be to help develop a geographic project for communities in the twenty-first century using a spatial-economic logic that puts at the forefront the idea of the commons.

# Chapter 10

# Beyond The Post-Industrial City? The Third Industrial Revolution, Digital Manufacturing and the Transformation of Homes into Miniature Factories

*John R. Bryson, Jennifer Clark and Rachel Mulhall*

The late spring 2013 issue of the *SkyMall* shopping catalogue heralded the emergence of the next technological or industrial revolution. The *SkyMall* catalogue is found on nearly every US flight and provides travelers with an opportunity to consider purchasing a range of new and novel products whilst onboard the aircraft. The late spring issue contains a $1,299 3D printer. 3D printers can be traced back to 1984, when stereolithography was developed by Charles Hull. This printing process enables a tangible 3D object to be created from digital data. The *SkyMall* 3D printer is described as '[s]uper easy and simple to use. It works by building up plastic material in three dimensions to create a real object. It's ideal for home, classroom and office and creates prototypes, models, toys … the list is endless'.[1] The reference to home use highlights the ability of this technology to shift some manufacturing production from the factory to the home. It is worth noting that 3D printing can also involve printing with

---

1    *SkyMall*, Late Spring Catalogue (Phoenix: SkyMall, 2013), 9.

metal powders. Nearly everything can be printed, but there are restrictions in terms of size. For example, it is a simple process to print a new cover for a mobile phone at home, but it will never be practicable to print a complete car. This re-emergence of home-based manufacturing has important implications for cities, as it enables new forms of customized manufacturing to emerge. Home-based manufacturing is not a new process, but this new industrial revolution has the potential to return manufacturing to its roots within the home.

Before the first industrial revolution, manufacturing was distributed in homes through a system of outworkers or via a process based on small craft-based production.[2] In the medieval European city, manufacturing was not isolated from homes — manufacturing was a home-based activity that was often undertaken by women and children during the day and men during the winter. During the nineteenth century the City of Birmingham, developed as the British Empire's workshop of the world, but the history of manufacturing in this city commenced in homes.[3] During the sixteenth century Birmingham was 'a village of manufacturers'.[4] Coventry, another important British manufacturing city, developed as a location for the manufacture of watches and ribbons, but both were manufactured in homes rather than in factories. The term 'manufacturing' is misleading.

2  Thomas S. Ashton, *An Eighteenth-Century Industrialist: Peter Stubs of War-rington, 1756–1806* (Manchester: Manchester University Press, 1961); W. H. B. Court, *A Concise Economic History of Britain* (Cambridge: Cambridge University Press, 1965); Phyllis Deane, *The First Industrial Revolution* (Cambridge: Cambridge University Press, 1969); Marie B. Rowlands, *Masters and Men in the West Midlands Metalware Trades before the Industrial Revolution* (Manchester: Manchester University Press, 1975); Gillian Darley, *Factory* (London: Reaktion Books, 2003); John R. Bryson and Michael Taylor, 'Mutual Dependency, Diversity and Alterity in Production: Cooperatives, Group Contracting and Factories', in *Interrogating Alterity*, eds. D. Fuller, A.E. Jonas, and R. Lee, 75–94 (Farnham: Ashgate, 2010).

3  J.D. Chambers, *The Workshop of the World* (Oxford: Oxford University Press, 1961); Bryson and Taylor, 'Mutual Dependency, Diversity and Alterity in Production'.

4  Artifex and Opifex, *The Causes of Decay in a British Industry* (London: Longmans, Green & Co., 1907), 2.

It comes with the association of large factories, smoking chimneys, conveyor belts and production lines, but actually the term comes from the Latin '*manu factum*' or 'to make by hand'. Thus, 'manufacturing' has a much more complex meaning than an association between the production process and the factory. There are many ways in which products can be manufactured — from craft-based production through to the technical complexity of putting together a robot. Manufacturing also takes place in a variety of circumstances and contexts, differing widely in scale from factories to spare bedrooms.

It was only during the latter part of the eighteenth century that a division began to emerge between the place of work and the place of residence. This division was driven by a requirement to control labour, especially as technological developments were beginning to replace simple home-based machines with much more complex machine tools.[5] These new machine tools were expensive and required access to a source of power (water, charcoal, coal, etc.) and also a workforce who could be increasingly managed and controlled to escalate productivity. Gradually, manufacturing located in cottages and homes was replaced by small factories often constructed in back gardens, and eventually these were superseded by the emergence of large specialist factories.[6] The exact date of this transfer from manufacturing in homes to factories varies depending on the industrial sector and location. In Coventry (UK) the manufacture of ribbons during the late nineteenth century was still predominantly a home-based activity. A typical Coventry weaver's house, at this time, consisted of a three- story building with the top story used as the 'topshop' or weaving loft in which there would be two or three looms.[7]

The first industrial revolution is associated with the emergence of factory production, and much of this production was

---

5    Rowlands, *Masters and Men.*
6    Darley, *Factory.*
7    John M. Prest, *The Industrial Revolution in Coventry* (Oxford: Oxford University Press, 1960), 75.

located in urban areas close to a source of power and labour. The second industrial revolution was based on the application of a spatial division of labour that spread manufacturing around the world driven by a search for lower production costs. This phase is associated with the deindustrialization of developed market economies, the emergence of post-industrial cities and the shift of production to emerging markets.[8] However, there are debates emerging that posit the start of the 'third industrial revolution'.[9] Rifkin's third industrial revolution is founded upon 'a new convergence of communication and energy [...] [in which] hundreds of millions of people will produce their own green energy in their homes, offices, and factories and share it with each other in an "energy internet".[10] There is another important technological driver that has the potential to transform manufacturing and that is leading to a new industrial revolution which has the possibility to transform the geography of production. These new technologies include laser cutting and 3D printing or additive manufacturing, and are associated with the re-emergence of home-based manufacturing that has the potential to challenge the dominant post-industrial model. The future of our cities will be based on knowledge, information and new forms of manufacturing, and some of this activity will be undertaken in offices and factories, and some in homes.

This new technological driver is a key issue in the transformation of manufacturing and includes a number of related innovations that can all be classified under the term 'digital

---

8    J.R. Bryson, P.W. Daniels, and B. Warf, *Service Worlds: People, Organisations, Technologies* (London: Routledge, 2004); Barry Bluestone and Bennett Harrison, *The Deindustrialisation of America: Plant Closings, Community Abandonment, and the Dismantling Of Basic Industry* (New York: Basic Books, 1982); Peter Dicken, *Global Shift: Transforming the World Economy* (London: Sage, 2003); John R. Bryson and Grete Rusten, *Design Economies and the Changing World Economy: Innovation, Production and Competitiveness* (London: Routledge, 2011).

9    Jeremy Rifkin, *The Third Industrial Revolution: How Lateral Power Is Transforming Energy, The Economy, and the World* (New York: Palgrave MacMillan, 2011).

10   Ibid., 2.

manufacturing'. These new technologies have the potential to democratize manufacturing, as it can transfer the design and manufacture of particular products from monopoly capitalism to a form of distributed home-based, customized capitalism. This type of production will never replace the existing factory-based mass manufacturing, but provides an alternative means for the production of small, often customized products, as well as creative art. In this chapter, we explore the emergence of digital manufacturing with a particular focus on 3D printing or rapid prototyping, and the impact that this could have on home-based manufacturing and the post-industrial city.

## From subtraction to addition

The history of much manufacturing is based around subtractive methods in which material is removed by cutting, drilling and other forms of machining. Subtractive manufacturing has been supplemented by technological developments that have given rise to additive manufacturing techniques, rapid prototyping or 3D printing.[11] Additive manufacturing is a process in which a three-dimensional solid object is produced by laying down successive layers of material (liquid, powder or sheet materials) controlled by a digital file. The digital file can be produced by 3D computer-aided design (CAD), model data, CT and MRI scan data, and data created from 3D digitizing systems. The development of 3D printing means that it is now possible for components and products to be developed using CAD and printed using a 3D printer. 3D printing is currently used in the aerospace

---

11   T. Wohlers, *Wohlers Report: Rapid Prototyping & Tooling State of the Industry Annual Worldwide Progress Report* (Fort Collins: Wohlers Associates, 2001); Xue Yan and P. Gu, 'A Review of Rapid Prototyping Technologies and Systems', *Computer-Aided Design* 28, no. 4 (1996): 307–18; S. Kumar and J.P. Kruth, 'Composites by Rapid Prototyping Technology', *Materials and Design* 31 (2010): 850–56; Additive Manufacturing Special Interest Group, *Shaping Our National Competency in Additive Manufacturing: A Technology Innovation Needs Analysis Conducted by the Additive Manufacturing Special Interest Group for the Technology Strategy Board* (London: Technology Strategy Board, 2012).

industry to produce light- weight components, and in the medical devices industry to create customized dental implants, customized insoles that match patients' feet and also customized hip replacements.

Unlike many emerging technologies, such as nanotechnology and biotechnology, additive manufacturing is associated with manufacturing processes of both large and small firms. 3D printing has developed as a central process technology in the 'maker movement' with its focus on personalized, customized and craft-based production of consumer items such as jewelry and household goods. This relationship to the Do-It-Yourself (DIY) movement has connected additive manufacturing to e-retailing portals for craft-based production such as Etsy and the development of 'maker-spaces', such as those managed by TechWorks.[12] TechWorks provides access to manufacturing spaces, including access to tools and machines for small-scale producers to prototype and produce batch items. The emergence of these new, flexible and shared manufacturing spaces in cities, coupled with the expanding capabilities enabled by digital manufacturing and 3D printing, are beginning to alter the trajectory of urban manufacturing by enabling home-based makers to design new objects that can be printed either at home or by a specialist 3D printing company. Central to this new third industrial revolution is the emergence of distributed manufacturing facilitated by digital manufacturing and personalized or customized design.

Innovations in additive manufacturing have the potential to shift manufacturing production away from capital intensive mass production based in large plants to a network of distributed manufacturing facilities that would focus on the production of mass customized products. Additive manufacturing comes with a number of benefits and these include:

- A decrease in lead times from design to products ready for market.

---

12  For more information on Etsy or TechWorks, see www.etsy.com or www. sktechworks.ca.

- A resource-efficient approach with no wastage.
- The ability to customize products.
- No requirement for specialist tooling. This reduces the scale of capital investment required to manufacture products.
- New developments in additive manufacturing are associated with rapid production throughputs.
- Limited defective parts.
- Parts and products can be designed to optimism functionality rather than for effective subtractive manufacturing.
- The ability to develop a hybrid manufacturing process that combines the benefits associated with subtractive and additive manufacturing.
- The ability to produce parts with the same functionality as parts produced by subtractive manufacturing, but with fewer raw materials. These products are much lighter.
- New products that can only be made by additive manufacturing. The layer process enables the manufacture of very complex shapes and there are few geometric limitations compared to subtractive manufacturing.

There are a number of research challenges that need to be overcome with additive manufacturing; these include scaling up the additive manufacturing process and overcoming some difficulties with the surface finish of products produced by additive manufacturing. The cost of 3D printers is declining and very small firms, individuals, schools and artists are now able to afford to purchase small 3D printers. The *SkyMall* 3D printer is an excellent example of the spread of relatively inexpensive digital manufacturing technologies to homes and offices. Developments in additive manufacturing have the potential to transform manufacturing and to produce a new geography of manufacturing. In theory, additive manufacturing could eliminate the subcomponent section of the supply chain.[13] Thus, the emphasis would shift from cost-competition for the subcompo-

---

13   Jennifer Clark, *Working Regions: Reconnecting Innovation and Production in the Knowledge Economy* (London: Routledge, 2013).

nents to pre-production elements including: 1) product design, 2) process design (software) and 3) materials (especially quality and purity). Indeed, this shift would produce a very different production geography. In fact some manufacturing has already transferred from factories back to the home and maker spaces, enabling people to develop new products that can be printed at home or be printed by a specialist provider of 3D printing services.

These developments will affect the expiry of key patents, the formulation of less expensive materials and the creation of machines that print at fast speeds. 3D printing makes it possible to produce light-weight structures that are extremely strong and optimism the relationship between material content and performance. This should lead to the development of entirely new businesses and business models. It is possible to argue that additive manufacturing is the most important technological development in manufacturing since the introduction of CAD. Developments in additive printing mean that individuals and small firms will have the capability to develop, design and print new products. 3D printers are being developed for domestic use, and it should become possible for an individual to purchase a product file that enables them to print a product at home.

Contract providers of 3D printing services already exist, and increasingly individuals and firms will be able to purchase customized products that are printed locally. Individuals will be able to download a 3D file linked to a company which will then print the object. A good example of this type of 'service' is provided by Shapeways (a company based in New York) which provide 3D printing services on demand. This technological development makes it extremely simple to customize products and to alter the relationship between manufacturing and consumers. Technically-minded individuals will be able to develop products that might be tested by companies that specialist in selling products that can be printed at home or by a provider of 3D printing services. This could lead to warehouse inventory levels being significantly reduced as more products could be printed close to the point of consumption. There are also important sustainability and climate change implications associated with 3D printing, as it makes it possible to localize and customize the production of many manufactured products. This could lead to the development of a much more distributed geography of production, but with specific centers allocated for their design and development. In effect, places that retain integrated design and production capacities will benefit, especially those with experience of absorbing process innovations.[14]

## Conclusion — from the post-industrial city to home-based manufacturing

The emergence of post-industrial cities or the shift towards a service world was associated with the transfer of manufacturing to low-cost locations.[15] This transformed Western cities as their economies were increasingly based on property and land speculation, financial services and business and professional services.[16] Many of these new economic activities involved the management of fictitious capital — capital that only existed for these new service workers on balance sheets and had limited connections with real people or tangible products. The economic crisis that commenced in 2008 has challenged the emphasis placed in Western cities on services and led to a debate regarding the rebalancing of national economies towards manufacturing.

Technological developments and the emergence of digital manufacturing provide a new driver that is transforming manufacturing. This new technology has the potential to convert every home into a miniature factory. There are important limitations. At the moment, home-based digital fabrication is focused on the production of small products, toys and artworks. This still reflects a radical innovation, as before the introduction of 3D printing it was impossible to produce many of these prod-

---

14  Bryson and Rusten, *Design Economies and the Changing World Economy;* Clark, *Working Regions.*

15  Bryson, Daniels, and Warf, *Service Worlds.*

16  John R. Bryson, 'Obsolescence and the Process of Creative Reconstruction', *Urban Studies* 34, no. 9 (1997): 1439–58.

ucts in a home setting. Digital manufacturing enables people to design and develop new products at home and to customize existing products. Products can be created at home and their digital files sent anywhere over the Web. This offers possibilities for home-based design and development, but printing would be undertaken by specialist 3D printing firms. The development of maker spaces may address this gap by enabling the printing of products in shared workshop settings located close to the home. At present, however, they are not widely available.

We are at the start of a new technological era founded on combining digital fabrication with post-industrial, home-based workers. These new home-based workers may work elsewhere during the day but play with creating new products during the evening and at weekends. There could also be home workers who specialist in the creation of new digital files and are contracted to companies or working for themselves to produce new products as well as new art. Additive tooling will not exceed more traditional machine tools, but could support such tooling through the development of hybrid manufacturing that blends subtractive with additive techniques. The start of the 'third' industrial revolution is returning some forms of manufacturing to the home and to the city. New forms of home work are emerging that will go hand-in-hand with services and workers who are currently able to work from home. These changes have important implications for the design of our cities and homes — the home of the future must be digitally connected, but it must also provide the space to balance living with digital manufacturing.

Chapter 11

# Conspicuous Production
## Valuing the Visibility of Industry in Urban Re-Industrialisation

*Karl Baker*

## Introduction

A flurry of recent commentary calls for a renewed focus on wealthy countries 'making things'.[1] Such arguments are generally framed within discourses on national economic growth and ignore the spatial implications of re-industrialization. However, treating the promotion of industrial activities as a key component of spatially-oriented urban development strategies offers promises to broaden the range of benefits delivered by a revived manufacturing sector. In realizing this potential, the built form supporting industry requires careful consideration. Shifts toward consolidating industry within demarcated zones of utili-

---

1 Advocates look to the potential for manufacturing to 're-balance' economies (see Peter Marsh. 'Hopes for Growth in Manufacturing', *The Financial
Times,* May 29, 2011, https://next.ft.com/content/9627941a-8a13-11e0-beff-
00144feab49a); revive the fortunes of the 'hollowed-out' middle classes (see
Don Peck, 'Can the Middle Class Be Saved?', *The Atlantic,* September 2011,
http://www.theatlantic.com/magazine/archive/2011/09/can-the-middle-
class-be-saved/308600/); and spur innovation and productivity growth (see
Ha-Joon Chang, *Kicking Away the Ladder: Economic Development in Historical Perspective* [London: Anthem, 2002]).

tarian sheds in the urban periphery,[2] while converting historic inner-city industrial buildings for the service economy,[3] are problematic manifestations of conventional planning for industry in today's 'post-industrial' city.

In response to inadequate attention to the built environment supporting emerging urban industry, I argue for a particularly 'conspicuous' form of production that values the everyday visibility of industrial activities. I outline some key benefits from visible forms of industry and some supportive approaches to the planning and design of built environments. Firstly, however, it is worth briefly mentioning potential drivers of contemporary 're-industrialization' in cities to more precisely understand the types of production that might be made more 'conspicuous'.

## Drivers of urban re-industrialization

The revival of industry in post-industrial cities like London, Barcelona or Philadelphia will not involve a return to the modes of production or the built environment of nineteenth-century industrialization. A number of emerging trends suggest various pathways along which contemporary activities of manufacture, repair and craft may become more important elements of urban economies. Firstly, it is conceivable that the geographic dispersal of industry, both to rural locations and further afield to globalized facilities distant from consumer markets, may in some cases be reversed. Recent 're-shoring' of manufacturing in the United States points in this direction,[4] with a US$1 billion initiative by General Electric to re-shore household appliance manu-

---

2   Owen Hatherley, *A Guide to the New Ruins of Britain* (London: Verso, 2010).

3   S. Zukin, *Naked City: The Death and Life of Authentic Urban Places* (Oxford: Oxford University Press, 2010); S. Zukin, *Loft Living: Culture and Capital in Urban Change* (Baltimore: John Hopkins University Press, 1982).

4   'Coming Home', *The Economist*, January 19, 2013, http://www.economist. com/news/special-report/21569570-growing-number-american-compa- nies-are-moving-their-manufacturing-back-united.

facturing gaining widespread attention.[5] Secondly, advanced manufacturing technologies including '3D printing' and digital fabrication may facilitate a reorganization of the geography of production, with cost-effective smaller scale manufacturing facilities and 'mass-customization'[6] encouraging the integration of production within urban areas closer to consumer markets.[7] Finally, growing enthusiasm for craft and artisanal local manufacture may contribute to an expanded 'boutique manufacturing' sector that deliberately locates in close proximity to inner-city consumer markets.[8]

## Valuing visible industry

Whether urban re-industrialization means a growing craft sector or a relocation of mass manufacturing, the quality of the built environment supporting these activities can strengthen the benefits resulting from a revived industrial sector. Currently, urban manufacturing businesses often occupy locations that are

---

5   Ed Crooks, 'GE Takes $1bn Risk in Bringing Jobs Home', *Financial Times,* April 2, 2012, https://next.ft.com/content/21a46546-78f1-11e1-88c5-00144feab49a.

6   'Mass customization' has gained currency as a concept in business and management literature since the early 1990s. For instance, see Joseph B. Pine II, *Mass Customization: The New Frontier in Business Competition* (Boston: Harvard Business School Press, 1993). Jane Jacobs makes a much earlier reference to the idea in Jane Jacobs, *The Economy of Cities* (London: Jonathon Cape, 1969), 245: 'Mass-production manufacturing will no longer be regarded as city work. Cities will manufacture even more goods than they do today, but these will be almost wholly differentiated production goods, made in relatively small, or very small, organizations'.

7   Neil Gershenfeld, 'How to Make Almost Anything: The Digital Fabrication Revolution', *Foreign Affairs* 91, no. 6 (2012): 43–57.

8   Recently formed advocacy organizations in a number of North American cities promote the potential of expanding urban artisanal production (alongside a broader interest in all forms of urban manufacturing) and include San Francisco-based SFMade, and Made in NYC. Examples of craft manufacturing in these cities include inner-city breweries, apparel, jewelry and furniture producers. See A. Arieff. 'The Future of Manufacturing Is Local', *The New York Times,* March 27, 2011, http://opinionator.blogs.nytimes.com/2011/03/27/the-future-of-manufacturing-is-local/?_r=0.

far from 'conspicuous'. While advanced 're-shored' manufacturing may return to urban rather than rural areas, it will most likely occupy sheds in segregated industrial zones. Artisanal manufacturing may be similarly hidden, using low-cost spaces in dilapidated remnants of nineteenth-century industrial buildings. Against this invisibility, a built environment that explicitly prioritizes public connections to industry can bring benefits in raising awareness of production processes, enabling social engagement between producers and the public and enriching everyday experiences of being in the public spaces of the city.

## Awareness

Industry that is publicly visible supports a range of connections between consumers and producers of manufactured goods. For example, a furniture maker with its production process open to a busy street, or even a car factory with manufacturing visible to passing motorists, can connect passers-by to the processes of manufacturing. This visual presence of production can prompt understanding of the human labor,[9] mechanical processes and energy required to produce the often taken-for-granted material goods of our industrial society.[10] Eco-localists refer to the IMBY (in my back yard) effect of local production in establishing an everyday awareness of the human and environmental costs of

---

9   Richard Sennett's celebration of 'The Craftsman' sees this archetypal figure as representing 'the special human condition of being engaged': Richard Sennett, *The Craftsman* (New Haven: Yale University Press, 2008), 20. The visibility of the human work and practical skill of the craftsman might be 'honored' and 'acknowledged' in the public realm.

10  The visibility of local production can help counter the 'alienation' of urban consumers from distant 'manufacturing hinterlands' — somewhat analogous to the alienation from distant ecological hinterlands obscured by infrastructural networks for food, energy and water. See Stephen Graham (ed.), *Disrupted Cities: When Infrastructure Fails* (London: Routledge, 2009); N. Heynen, M. Kaika, and E. Swyngedouw, *In the Nature of Cities: Urban Political Ecology and the Politics of Urban Metabolism* (London: Routledge, 2006); Maria Kaika, *City of Flows: Modernity, Nature and the City* (New York: Routledge, 2005).

production,[11] and the possibility of more considered consumption behaviors.[12] At the same time, more public forms of production might act as a form of quality assurance, pressuring businesses to improve their environmental and social performance.

## Social/economic engagement

Beyond establishing a visual awareness of production processes among urban consumers, some forms of industry can also allow for social engagement through economic exchanges between makers and buyers. Small-scale industries supplying local customers illustrate the possibilities of these types of relationships. Referring to 'Reyd's Bespoke Tailor Shop' in London, Suzanne Hall describes the 'respect' that emerges in the direct encounter between producers and consumers:

> This form of respect — the reciprocal recognition between maker and wearer — of the skill involved in making a bespoke garment is not a social relation that can exist in off-the-peg fashion stores, where the product on display is separated from its process of making.[13]

These relationships of respect and 'reciprocal recognition' add a richness to social experiences not possible within conventional consumer-retailer exchanges based around the sale of goods made in distant hinterlands. Furthermore, these direct connections with makers can strengthen local economies by orienting consumer spending toward local manufacturers rather than multinational corporations.

---

11  Fred Curtis, 'Eco-Localism and Sustainability', *Ecological Economics* 46 (2003): 83–102, at 93.

12  Colin Hines, *Localization: A Manifesto* (London: Earthscan, 2000), 35.

13  Suzanne Hall, *City, Street and Citizen: The Measure of the Ordinary* (London: Routledge, 2012), 86.

## Rich and distinctive urban experiences

The visibility and presence of industrial activities in the spaces of everyday life can provide rich and distinctive experiences for city dwellers. Stronger connections between productive processes and public space can contribute to a fuller sensory experience of urban life that counters the 'erosion of the perceptual sphere' accompanying too much 'sanitized' urban re-development.[14] The activity of industry, including the noise, smells and rhythms of human and mechanical production can be celebrated for the diversity and interest that they bring to city streets. While there may be conflict over what is treated as 'nuisance' or as adding vitality to the street, recent urbanism may well have gone too far in attempting to eliminate sensory confrontation. At worst, current post-industrial spatial conditions involve a sterile monotony of glass office and retail frontages in prime spaces of the city, and the relegation of industry to equally monotonous sheds in well-defined suburban industrial parks. A re-industrialization that celebrates what Jane Jacobs termed the 'jumble' of the diverse and truly mixed-use street,[15] can contribute to more distinctive and intriguing urban experiences.

Visible forms of urban industry can further make everyday experiences of being in the city more meaningful by connecting public life with the activities going on 'behind the scenes' of building frontages. Connecting the public realm with that of workplaces is a challenge not only for industrial activities, but also for the hidden and disconnected work done in offices. Making work more visible increases the legibility of the city and might introduce other ways of being in public — or loosely among others — in ways that are different to dominant modes of consumption-based public space.[16]

---

14  Mirko Zardini (ed.), *Sense of the City: An Alternative Approach to Urbanism* (Baden: Lars Müller Publishers, 2005), 21.

15  Jane Jacobs, *The Death and Life of American Cities* (New York: Modern Library, 1961).

16  Steven Miles, *Spaces for Consumption: Pleasure and Placelessness in the Post-Industrial City* (London: Sage, 2010); Demos, *People Make Place: Growing*

## Spatial planning and design for visible urban industry

Encouraging the visibility of industry requires a particular approach to spatial planning and design. It raises questions across scales about how different spatial arrangements — from the planning of urban regions to the configuration of rooms in a building — impact on the everyday visibility of industry. In the following section, I outline two elements of spatial policy and design that may support the emergence of a more conspicuous form of production.

### Beyond industrial zones

Urban-planning conventions that emerged from historical responses to the noxious 'nuisances' of nineteenth-century industrialization have resulted in regulating-out particularly polluting or noisy industries from the densely inhabited parts of cities in advanced economies.[17] Zoning regulations have encouraged remaining industrial activities (even those with limited external impacts) to locate in demarcated industrial areas, often deliberately segregated from the spaces of everyday urban life. While this approach continues to make sense for a range of heavy industries, the type of activities driving contemporary re-industrialization, such as digital fabrication and craft, are relatively clean and quiet, and their placement in the city should not be determined by planning approaches based on exclusive land-use zoning.

Even current urban-planning strategies that encourage urban industrial activities continue to favor approaches based on the continuation of segregated industrial zones. In London, for instance, industrial land is valued by official planning policy, but

the Public Life of Cities (London: Demos, 2005); Susan Christopherson, 'The Fortress City', in Post-Fordism: A Reader, ed. A. Amin, 409–25 (Oxford: Blackwell, 1995).

17 The amelioration of negative impacts from industry has been central to the historical development of urban spatial planning practices. See Paul Hall, Cities of Tomorrow: An Intellectual History of Urban Planning and Design in the Twentieth Century (Oxford: Basil Blackwell, 1988).

policy also attempts to consolidate industry in large-scale de-marcated areas, predominantly on the outskirts of the city and less visible to everyday public life. This is despite 60 per cent of all industrial land being located in small parcels dispersed throughout the city—behind the high street or in neighbor-hood workshops.[18]

Alternative spatial policies could encourage dispersed ar-rangements of small industrial zones throughout the urban re-gion. Better still, land-use zoning could be relaxed to allow light industrial activities to co-exist with other uses in more broadly defined mixed-use zones.[19] These types of policies could create a more visible form of industry through integration and mix-ing with residential and commercial uses.[20] Such policies could bring industry closer to the spaces of urban residents' everyday lives, allowing for more accessible connections between con-sumers and producers, and between people's homes and indus-trial workplaces.

## Transparent factories

Spatial planning at the city scale is essential for allowing new and existing industrial activities to locate in places closely con-nected with the public life of the city. Planning at the city scale is not, by itself, sufficient to ensure the everyday visibility of in-dustry. The design of individual buildings and the relationship between industrial activities and the public spaces of the street are also important for realizing the benefits of conspicuous pro-duction.

---

18 Greater London Authority, *Supplementary Planning Guidance: Industrial Capacity* (London: Greater London Authority, 2008), 34.

19 A change of industrial-zoning categories and introduction of industrial mixed-use zones has been recommended in Philadelphia in the United States. See Philadelphia Industrial Development Corporation, *An Industrial Market and Land Use Strategy for the City of Philadelphia — Executive Sum-mary* (2010), 17, http://www.pidcphila.com/images/uploads/resource_li-brary/PIMLUS_Executive_Summary_Final_September_2010.pdf.

20 As documented with some examples from London in Urhahn Urban De-sign, *Industry in the City: A Report for the London Development Agency and Greater London Authority* (Amsterdam: Urhahn Urban Design, 2010).

Visible industry need not involve extremes of 'transparent factories',[21] but consideration of how industrial activities might contribute to the public life of the city deserves more attention. It is rare for current planning policy to place value on the form of industrial buildings, even in cases where policy pays careful attention to the provision of industrially-zoned land.[22]

In imagining contemporary re-industrialization based on high-tech manufacturing, distributed digital fabrication and the revival of craft, there are various ways in which these activities might be made publicly visible. For instance, a degree of permeability in the interface between public and private space is important in connecting interior production spaces with exterior public life. Rather than industrial premises having blank walls facing streets or being located along back alleys, industry could be valued for its contribution to achieving conventional urban design objectives of vibrant streets and active ground-floor frontages.

It is easy to imagine street-level workshops with open windows and doors allowing glimpses of craft-type activities to passers-by. Furthermore, hybrid making-selling spaces can provide an intermediate semi-public retail space that directly links producers with consumers. Simple design features at the building scale can expand the scope for interaction between industrial producers and the urban public. Open windows, large doorways and opportunities for signage are all useful. Likewise, it is important to prevent careless and inflexible design that often characterizes ground-floor commercial spaces in contemporary residential-led 'mixed-use' development. Awkward transitions between public and private spaces created by changes of level, steps and fences all prevent interaction between building and

---

21  The name given to Volkswagon's glass-clad car assembly plant in Dresden, Germany, constructed in 1992 and open for public tours.

22  See, for example, progressive urban industrialization strategies including Philadelphia Industrial Development Corporation, *An Industrial Market and Land Use Strategy*, 17; Nisha Mistry, *Newark's Manufacturing Competitiveness* (Washington, DC: Brookings Institute, 2013), https://www.brookings.edu/wp-content/uploads/2016/06/NewarkManufacturingMay28.pdf.

street, and reduce the flexibility of spaces for industrial uses. Exposing larger-scale mechanical, rather than craft, processes of production may present more challenges and may not offer businesses the same advantages from direct links with consumers. Nevertheless, heightened visibility of such processes still has benefits for the legibility of the city, and exposing these types of activities may offer exciting design opportunities.

## Further questions

This chapter has sketched an argument for the importance of paying attention to the built form that will support any future urban re-industrialization. Specifically, the concept of 'conspicuous production' is used to suggest ways in which the spatial planning of cities and the design of buildings accommodating industrial uses can support the public visibility and integration of industry within mixed-use urban environments. A number of questions emerge from this brief discussion and deserve a mention. Firstly, the benefits of visible industry have in this chapter been framed primarily around advantages to a 'consuming public'. It will be important to further investigate how visibility benefits producers themselves, especially when inconspicuousness may often be a deliberate strategy for manufacturers who may wish to avoid public scrutiny. Secondly, in focusing on advantages to the public life of cities, this chapter has not dealt with a range of other benefits from re-industrialization, including employment, environmental and energy-use implications, and the promise of innovation and other economic advantages arising from urban production. Expanded versions of this chapter will need to consider how the concept of visibility may complement these arguments. Finally, while the chapter deliberately focussed on the reform of spatial and built environment conditions as a neglected aspect of the re-industrialization argument, a consideration of changes to politico-economic and institutional conditions will be equally important in realizing the promise of industry in the city.

Chapter 12

# Industri[us]
# Re/Use, Re/Work, Re/Value

*Christina Norton*

## Intoducing Industri[us]

This chapter explores Industri[us], an initiative that was set up
in early 2011 by 'Fluid' (architects and urban strategists) and
collaborators in order to highlight the growing opportunity of
upcycling[1] and its uses in urban regeneration and sustainable
development. To begin, I explain the concept of Industri[us],
its motives and its relationship to the theme of re-industrialization and progressive urbanism. I also discuss and present the
'Festival of Up-Cycling' in Canning Town which was delivered
from May to September 2012 and was a prototype and test case
for how up-cycling can contribute towards sustainable development and have a role in urban regeneration.

The basic premise of Industri[us] is to put a vacant site to creative interim use in advance of commercial development taking
place. To do this requires collaboration with the growing community of designers and makers working with waste materials
and needing better access to the market; the resulting network
connects with a supply of waste materials, as well as providing

---

1   Up-cycling is the making of desirable goods from waste materials — i.e.,
    items and materials that people and industries throw away.

a series of innovation and education programs. This approach to making use of essentially 'useless' and time- limited land is a reaction to a consideration of what isn't working in cities today, in particular looking at high streets and town centers, and considering how improvements could be made through reflecting on social, economic and environmental values and transformations. It is also a response to the increasing loss of industrial activity from the urban condition and the steady movement towards a mono-cultural city. The project also seeks to enable communities to take ownership and control of their environment, address inequality, move towards self-sufficiency and, through participation and occupation, foster notions of public space that are both relevant and successful.

'Fluid' works at the threshold between architecture, planning and creative practice, having been involved in urban projects since the 1990s and having developed a process of dynamic planning that is driven by community engagement and participation. The act of design engages with the social and cultural as well as the physical and is seen as a service, not just a product. The work engages with the macro-, meso- and micro-scales, linking big strategic thinking with small scale-change and intervention, believing that the things that really influence and affect the city are those at the level of infrastructure and human interaction. Industri[us] signifies an intent that has multiple readings: the connection with Industry and heritage, the idea of making and doing, the notion of hard work and the fact that we do it.

## Objectives

Industri[us] is about helping communities to get back on their feet and thrive. Through injecting short-term activity into an unused site and creating new businesses and jobs by harnessing waste as an economic opportunity, it seeks to bring about positive longer-term social, economic and environmental changes. As well as setting out to revalue waste materials, Industri[us] places the provision of training opportunities to help people into employment and to connect the communities that are at the centre of its operations. Through this, a lasting skills base is built, strengthening local networks and raising aspirations. It is becoming widely accepted that to move towards a more sustainable urban environment, our future high streets and town centers must be multi-functional social and cultural 'institutions'. To achieve this aim, a variety of changes need to occur that encourage activity, interaction and a range of experiences that are rooted in the interests and needs of local people and that provide opportunities and the infrastructure for local enterprise to support local institutions and meet the demands for a flexible and innovative move towards change. By encouraging local innovation and cultural expression and being a platform for creating new businesses, Industri[us] aims to directly addresses these objectives to re-think town centers in an economically sustainable way, creating a destination for a wider audience. At the same time, the project strongly promotes the ambitions of a 'low-carbon economy' through self-sufficiency and local economies creating projects entirely from borrowed, used or re-usable materials.

## Value

Industri[us] is a place of work, making, learning, playing, exchange, trade and interaction that offers a new model for the development of existing high streets. The value of 'meanwhile' is an underused resource in planning and development, offering critical creativity, opportunity and sustainability. Instead of top-down masterplanning, the 'meanwhile' idea involves a more dynamic approach, working across disciplines in order to test and seed change for the long-term legacy of a site. This dynamism means exploring new forms of practice that cross boundaries between architecture, planning and art: such a collaborative method expands to include wider community participation in order to negotiate the social, economic and cultural aspects of the site. Investigating and animating vacant sites, the 'meanwhile' idea is as much about the space in between as the time in between. More usually, these spaces are located in areas of transition, which itself generates creative enterprise and experimentation.

One of the ways Industri[us] attempts to engage with vacant sites and the local community is through The Meanwhile Project. The aim of this project is to provide opportunities for design in its broadest sense, with the architect acting as an agent of change. It is a narrative and situation-based form of design where the ordinary can be transformed into the extraordinary. The process itself is as important as the product, comprised of illuminating moments of exchange, achievement, insight and learning, aimed at enabling and empowering communities and stakeholders.

## The Up-cycling context

The scale of waste produced in London is vast. Of the 3,860,000 tonnes generated in 2009 to 2010, 68% went to landfill or for incineration and just 32% for recycling or reuse. Only 6,000 tonnes of waste were diverted away from landfill by reuse organizations in 2011; 40,000 tonnes is the Mayor's target for 2015. A lot needs to be done to raise the profile and practice of reuse and up-cycling to hit this target.

Neither the current nor the potential value of the up-cycling market are easy to quantify because, as an emerging industry, figures are not readily available. However, both the National Industrial Symbiosis Programme (NISP) in the UK and Chicago's Waste-to-Profit Network are demonstrating the capacity of waste and reuse to create new enterprises and employment; including old tyres turned into playground mats, restaurant cooking oils turned into biodiesel, old uniforms turned into bags and glass scraps turned into countertops. Despite the economic downturn, the picture for emerging creative and innovative businesses looks relatively good.

Meanwhile, the financial gain to manufacturers of putting their waste to new use is known to be considerable. Established brands such as Freitag and new brands such as Styling & Salvage have entered the retail mainstream. In addition, there are an increasing number of high-profile events focusing on fashion reuse, such as 'super-swish' clothes swaps. The emerging market for up-cycled goods demonstrates that such products can generate considerable value and that people are buying into the idea of 'something created out of nothing'. Industri[us] aims to foster this creative transformation by providing enterprise opportunities for existing up-cyclers and facilitating others to enter the industry. It also creates a 'hub' by drawing together like-minded groups and through this critical mass forming a destination.

## An 'engine of change'

Conceived as a production line in an 'engine of change', populated by an evolving coalition of artists, entrepreneurs, social businesses, mentors and local people who all realize the value of waste, the concept of Industri[us] in practice is made up of three elements: the Engine Room, the Makeshift Market and the Spotlight. The Industri[us] production line begins with the delivery and collection of materials suitable for reuse — from individuals, schools, markets, manufacturers — before they become part of the conventional waste disposal chain. The Engine Room is the brain of the Industri[us] operation and home to a range of innovative producers — from start-ups and those in need of a launch pad, to existing enterprises looking to expand or to co-locate with others working in material reuse. Workshop spaces are provided for carpentry, jewelry-making and other small-scale fabrication; while training and mentoring are offered for start-up creative businesses, linked with local professionals and groups through partnership schemes. Community groups and schools can come to the Engine Room for hands-on activities and learning.

Completed products are then delivered to the Makeshift Market — the Industri[us] 'shopfront'. Here, products from the Engine Room workshops and other makers are displayed and sold in an 'arcade' — a demountable structure built from reused materials. Visitors can also learn workshop skills or how to 'make-do-and-mend', whilst also enjoying food stalls and out-door entertainments. A central 'think space' provides an ideas forum and an ad hoc research base for up-cycling, while smaller spaces are available for themed activities and discussions. By offering up-cycled fashion, furniture, art and accessories — at competitive prices — Makeshift attracts a particular but grow-ing type of consumer. It is a shopping destination, as well as a beacon of creative enterprise and green innovation, with the potential to be replicated on other sites. A variety of entertain-ment events staged at Makeshift attempts to draw in a wider au-dience and additional revenue, from makers' fairs and fashion shows to fun science activities and DIY workshops. A weekly, seasonal and potentially annual calendar of events is the next stage of development and is established and curated by the local Industri[us] team.

The final part of the production line involved in Industri[us] is Spotlight. Spotlight is a place for public spectacle, with large-scale installations designed to make people think twice about the nature of 'waste'. A dynamic large-scale installation, Spot-light acts as a highly visible signpost for Industri[us] and aims to prompt people to rethink the nature of waste.

## The Festival of Up-Cycling

Industri[us] first came to life through the Meanwhile London 'Festival of Up-Cycling' in Canning Town in the Olympic sum-mer of 2012. Developed in collaboration with local organiza-tions and delivery partners, the Festival provided work experi-ence and paid training opportunities for young people and the long-term unemployed. It also supported existing up-cycling businesses and start-ups, making and selling products from fur-niture and art to jewelry and fashion in order to create a show-case and model for enterprise. The project was created entirely from borrowed, used or reusable materials, including pavers from the nearby Olympics roadworks to plants, materials and whole gardens reused from the Chelsea Flower Show. Two tem-porary public squares were created on the Canning Town site, along with a street 'pop-up' food market and a striking scaffold-ing pavilion to house an up-cycling market and other associated events.

Industri[us] at Canning Town had two starting points — the amount of waste produced by or traveling through the London Borough of New ham (towards wharves for onward transporta-tion to landfill sites) and the growing 'community of interest' in up-cycling (both locally and regionally) — turning waste mate-rials and products into desirable and valuable objects for use and sale. This dovetailed with the Greater London Authority's (GLA's) vision for a Green Enterprise District, lead by the arrival of Siemens in the Royal Docks. In 2009 to 2010, only 15 percent of Newham's waste went for recycling or reuse. However, the future looks brighter with the growth of local social enterprises promoting community recycling and generating employment through the resale of used products.

The Festival of Up-Cycling gathered together makers, doers, traders and show people to create a destination through critical mass. It provided support and links with other green enterprise initiatives in the area and hosted a Green Pioneers Conference with the London Borough of Newham, University of East Lon-don and Happold Consulting. The exchange that occurred at the festival through training and skilling in studios and workspaces brought with it the notion of the prosumer and reintroduced the world of making at the heart of a neighborhood. Newham is one of the most deprived boroughs in London, with unemployment rates at double the national average and almost a quarter of the population without qualifications or workplace skills training. However, with the UK's largest population of under-twenty-five-year-olds,[2] it was through the staging of the Festival that the op-portunity to tap into and help train a wealth of dormant talent was realized.

The Festival of Up-Cycling officially launched on July 27, 2012 and, coinciding with the start of the London 2012 Olympic

---

2   Figures sourced from NEF report on the 2012 Games and East London, April 2008.

Games, closed in early September. Located on Silvertown Way and opposite Canning Town Station, the site fronted onto the Olympics Spectator Walking Route which led down to ExCel. By day the Canning Town Giant, constructed entirely from reclaimed wood from local businesses, and designed and erected by the Robot Art collective with help from local youth group Peacock Gym, created a local icon and visual marker for the project. By night, the Makeshift pavilion became an illuminated beacon.

A broad audience was sought from those with an interest in reuse and design, to those who wished to buy their lunch from the street food market, or to explore the makeshift market and showcase of up-cycled design and local goods for sale. A number of live music nights were staged, which attracted audiences from the local area and further afield. During its time in operation, the Festival supported a number of existing up-cycling businesses and start-ups, who make and sell products from furniture and art to jewelry and clothing.

## Conclusion

Industri[us] is as much about the process of transformation as about an end result. So its short operational time was not as important as the fact that ten young local trainees gained employment following their involvement. Although the makeshift market structure was dismantled in September 2012, 'Fluid' handed over the license for the site to their partners, Groundwork UK, who have continued to operate it as a Reuse Centre, supporting community events such as car-boot sales and retaining the Giant Canning Town Robot. In 2013, the site again received planting and materials from the Chelsea Flower Show continuing the landscaping of the large site to create a positive public garden whilst providing training and routes into employment for the under-skilled and long-term unemployed.

Industri[us] has inspired many other projects and has been used as a best-practice example for the development of interim-use strategies as part of regeneration processes, including informing Olympic Legacy projects.

# Chapter 13

# Working with the Neighbors Cooperative Practices Delivering Sustainable Benefits

*Kate Royston*

In our fast-moving, goal-driven society it's easy to be insular, but considerable benefits can be gained from talking to, and working with, the neighbors. This can be particularly true across port industrial areas. Ports and their related industrial and amenity areas are critical economic and social components in their region. As hubs for industry, business, leisure and logistics, they are also resource-intensive and can pose environmental and social challenges. In the Netherlands, ports are vital to the national economy. Faced with increasing growth, limited space and ever-tightening environmental constraints, innovative collaborative solutions have had to be developed to support port areas' intensification. One approach is industrial ecological thinking.

## Industrial Ecology Thinking

Industrial ecology examines the way in which industrial systems can mimic natural systems, and in so doing reduce their impact on, and increase their harmony with, the natural environment. In natural systems, materials are part of closed cycles or circular systems. Industrial ecology seeks to take a systematic approach to the 'management of materials and energy flows through the human economy, including beneficial use of waste'.[1]

Understanding the materials, energy, water and other resources being consumed to produce products and services is an important starting point for systematically looking at how industrial systems and processes can be re-designed, costs reduced and new opportunities grasped. Importantly, this could also support the pro-active management of the risks and vulnerabilities we face from reducing resource availability.

## IE evolution across Dutch Port areas

The practice of IE across Dutch port areas appears to have evolved from the Rotterdam area facilitated by a history of business association (now represented by Deltalinqs), catalyzed in the late 1990s by government support to extend environmental improvement beyond mere compliance.[2]

## IE and the Port of Rotterdam

A suggestion to test some of the lessons from Kalundborg in Denmark, where inter-firm co-operation began in the early 1980s, led to the start of the Industrial EcoSystem (INES) project in 1994. A long-running project, INES gave rise to a number of influential co-operative opportunities which continue to evolve today. These include the Botlek steam-pipe network, with the

1   Roland Clift, 'Clean Technology and Industrial Ecology', in *Pollution: Causes, Effects and Control*, ed. R.M. Harrison, 411–44 (Cambridge: The Royal Society of Chemistry, 2001).

2   René van Berkel, 'Regional Resource Synergies for Sustainable Development in Heavy Industrial Areas: An Overview of Opportunities and Experiences', 2009, https://www.researchgate.net/publication/270340749_Regional_Resource_Synergies_for_Sustainable_Development_in_Heavy_Industrial_Areas_an_Overview_of_Opportunities_and_Experiences; Frank Boons, 'Self-Organisation & Sustainability: The Emergence of a Regional Industrial Ecology', *Emergence: Complexity and Organization* 10, no. 2 (2008): 40–47, https://journal.emergentpublications.com/article/self-organization-and-sustainability-the-emergence-of-a-regional-industrial-ecology/.

potential to save 400,000 tonnes of $CO_2$ per annum and deliver air-quality improvement, currently under construction.[3]

Now considered normal practice across the port industrial area, IE principles have been incorporated within the design of Maasvlakte II, the newest development area of the port, which will be serviced through the provision of centralized utilities.[4] Significant benefit is also being derived from the Organic $CO_2$ for Assimilation of Plants (OCAP) initiative, supplying 500 horticultural businesses over 1,600 hectares with residual $CO_2$ from Shell Pernis.[5] The horticulturists benefit from production and quality improvements and stable supply prices and are able to save 95 million cubic meters ($m^3$)/per annum (pa) of natural gas and 170,000 tonnes/pa of $CO_2$ emissions.[6]

## Port of Moerdijk

The Port of Moerdijk, a leading light in eco-industrial park development, has evolved from its beginnings as a petrochemical cluster. Established in the 1970s to link Shell Moerdijk via pipelines to Shell Pernis (Rotterdam), there are numerous material flows between Shell and other cluster organizations.

In 1994, a study of environmental practices initiated by the provincial government led to an action plan to redevelop the area as an eco-industrial estate, beginning with collaborative environmental monitoring.[7] Progress has been supported through

---

3   Rotterdam Climate Initiative, *Full Steam Ahead! Rotterdam Climate Initiative: 2008 Report — Summary* (Rotterdam: Rotterdam Climate Initiative, 2009), http://www.rotterdamclimateinitiative.nl/documents/ samenvatting%20Op%20Stoom%20EN.pdf; Port of Rotterdam, 'Port Wants Steam Pipe For $CO_2$ Reduction', November 22, 2009, http://www.portofrotterdam.com/en/News/pressreleases-news/Pages/20091126_01.aspx.

4   Port of Rotterdam, 'Innovative Use of Space Looking for Environmental Advantages', 2016, https://www.maasvlakte2.com/en/index/show/id/696/sustainable-layout.

5   OCAP, *$CO_2$ voor de tuinbouw — Factsheet 2012*, 2012, http://www.ocap.nl/files/Ocap_Factsheet2012_UK.pdf

6   Ibid.

7   Haven van Moerdijk, 'Port of Moerdijk', 2016, http://www.havenschapmoerdijk.nl/en/. Haven Amsterdam, 'Port of Amsterdam'; Harmen Veldman, personal communication to author, August 31, 2011.

Fig. 1: Sustainable Links at Moerdijk. Source: Moerdijk Port Authority. *Key*: red dashed line — potential connections for residual heat, energy, water and $CO_2$; white solid line — existing connections; yellow 'hatched' area — expansion area (132 ha) for a chemical industry cluster

a multi-party steering group, with the businesses represented by their association (BIM). The Port Authority acts as co-ordinator and facilitator.[8]

Over time, an increasing number of beneficial relationships have developed. Shell, the anchor tenant, supports a number of residual flows, including steam with the co-sited municipal incineration plant (Afvalverbranding Zuid-Nederland — AZN) and co-generation plant (Essent), and $CO_2$ is piped to Omya (a neighbouring business — see fig. 1) where it is used, together with $CO_2$ from NV Slibverwerking Noord-Brabant's sewage sludge incineration, in the production of calcium carbonate.

---

8    René van Berkel, 'Regional Resource Synergies'; Haven van Moerdijk, 'Port of Moerdijk'.

A further detailed resource-flow assessment across the area identified more potential linkages and established the 'Sustainable Links Moerdijk' (fig. 1) program. Supported by an enabling agreement and funding instruments, it includes a vision to implement an 'Energyweb' across the area, which is now well underway.

## Zeeland Seaports

At Zeeland Seaports, well-established industries such as Dow Chemicals have capitalized upon their residual resource streams through symbiotic linkages which have evolved over time; for example, pipelines have replaced haulage between Cargill and Nedalco. The importance of these connections was recognized by Zeeland Seaports and other stakeholders, and Valuepark Terneuzen (VPT) and Biopark Terneuzen (BPT) were established in 2007.[9]

BPT's aim is to attract more agro-industrial businesses supported by 'smart links' to interconnect resource streams (fig.2).[10] This would enable a 'plug-and-play' offer to be made to new businesses, reducing the risk for the new entrant as well as enabling diversification for the port. The feasibility of the deployment of implementing a Multi-User Provider (MUP) pipeline concept across the whole area is being explored as part of the EU project Ports Adapting To Change (PATCH);[11] and a pilot joint venture, Warmco, has been set up to deliver heat and 70,000 tonnes pa of $CO_2$ to a new development of horticultural produc-

9  Partners include Cargill, Nedalco, Yara, EcoServices, ESV Groep, Heros Groep, Rosendaal Energy, Valuepark Terneuzen (JV Zeeland Seaports & Dow Benelux), Gemeente Terneuzen, Provincie Zeeland and Zeeland Seaports Port Authority.

10  D. Engelhardt, 'Sustainability in the Bio/Agro Industry: A Case Study', *Institute of Civil Engineers* 163, no. 1 (2010): 3–8, http://www.icevirtuallibrary.com/doi/pdf/10.1680/warm.2010.163.1.3

11  H. Holt, *The Art of Green Patchwork: European Ports Collaborate to Innovate Ports Adapting To Change (PATCH)*, GreenPort, 2011; http://www.zeelandseaports.nl/nl/download/file:green-patchwork.htm

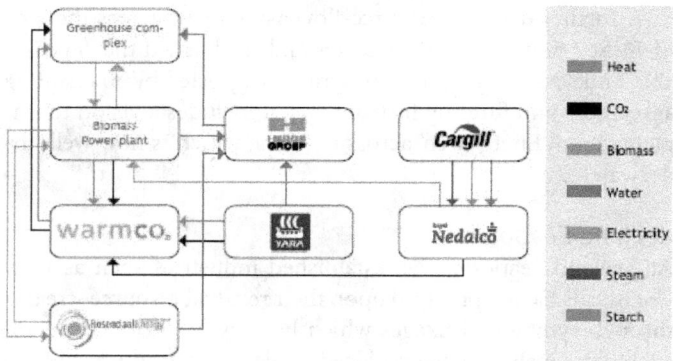

Fig. 2: Biopark Terneuzen Smart links. *Key: hitte* = heat, *biomassa* = biomass, *electriciteit* = electricity, *stoom* = steam, *zetmeel* = starch. Source: Biopark Terneuzen, Benefits for business and the environment, Biopark Terneuzen, 2012, http://www.bioparkterneuzen.com/nl/download/file:drieluikfolder-biopark-2012.htm.

ers. The co-operation also extends across the border with the Ghent Bio Energy Valley in Belgium to form Bio Base Europe.[12]

## Port of Amsterdam

A number of initiatives at the Port of Amsterdam (PoA) have evolved through its close links with the City government. Industrial ecology is seen as an important component in enabling the City and PoA to achieve their jointly set targets to reduce $CO_2$ emissions by 40 percent by 2025.[13]

---

12  D. Engelhardt, *Sustainability in the Bio/Agro Industry*; 'Bio Base Europe', 2011, http://www.biobaseeurope.eu/.

13  Roselin Dey, 'Amsterdam — Sustainable City in the Making', *Justmeans*, May 26, 2010, http://www.justmeans.com/blogs/amsterdam-sustainable-city-in-the-making; 'For a Clean Society', *The Amsterdam Energy Company* (AEB), 2016, http://www.aebamsterdam.com.

## The Amsterdam Energy Company

The Amsterdam Energy Company (AEB) is a PoA tenant, operated by the City of Amsterdam.[14] Its two incinerators are co-located with a waste water treatment plant. Feedstock includes municipal and commercial waste, and sewage sludge from the water treatment plant. 1 million MegaWatt Hours (MWh) electricity is output each year supplying the City, powering its tram and metro systems, street lighting and several buildings.[15] Further, Westport Warmte (WPW), a joint venture between the City and an energy company, takes heat from AEB and supplies local businesses and residents.[16]

Greenmills is also of interest. A partnership of businesses producing bio-diesel, bio-ethanol and bio-gas have co-located, taking in residual streams from port area food and animal feed producers and gaining logistical advantages and efficiency of resource use (including heat and water) through collaboration.[17] Surplus heat is distributed via a WPW connection,[18] A resource mapping project called 'Waste = Raw Materials in the Amsterdam harbors region' sponsored by the City and the Port Authority') also identified organic phosphorous which is being used by ICI Fertilizers.[19]

## Drivers, Enablers and Barriers

Industrial ecology is clearly an important factor in Dutch port development, for individual businesses and for the port estate and wider area as a whole. In Moerdijk, the co-operative practices have been particularly well-embedded within the area's

---

14 'Welcome to Amsterdam's Waste and Energy Company'.

15 J. Lammers, *Seaports as Turntables towards Sustainability: Policy Letter on Sustainable Seaports,* Directoraat-Generaal Luchtvaart en Maritieme Zaken, Ministerie van Verkeer en Waterstaat, 2008.

16 Haven van Amsterdam, 'Port of Amsterdam', 2011, http://www.portofamsterdam.nl/smartsite.dws?id=18493.

17 Ibid.

18 Ibid.; Veldman, personal communication to author.

19 Ibid.; Veldman, personal communication to author.

Fig. 3: Felixstowe Skip Trailer. *Source*: Port of Felixstowe

management and partnership structures. Whilst differences can be seen in their evolution (timing and approaches) there are a number of common factors. These were compared to practices in the UK through a research study across twenty port operations in Southwest England.[20] This highlighted that key drivers are much weaker. The strong Dutch regulatory pressure and government support to improve environmental conditions are less evident, whilst barriers are much in evidence. There is limited contact between businesses, and business associations linking neighbors to common aims are rare. Co-operation around common interests such as planning and development, through multi-stakeholder partnerships, is also uncommon, This limits chances to develop trusting relationships. The limited public stake in the port realm is also a factor.

There are opportunities, but these need enabling. The role of facilitators and champions, such as anchor tenants, are essential to develop and sustain interest; infrastructure for knowledge sharing and information exchange, technical assistance and, importantly, an economic business case are also important ingredients.

---

20  K. Royston, *Application of Industrial Ecology across Port Areas: The Potential to Leverage Commercial Advantage and Support Sustainable Development in SW England* (MSc Thesis, University of Surrey, 2011).

## Deepening collaboration over time

Research and practice show that collaboration can deepen over time from quick wins to wider co-operation as confidence grows between businesses. Larger infrastructure projects such as pipeline links may develop where the business case makes sense.

Quick wins are important for developing confidence between parties. They can be facilitated through tools, such as National Industrial Symbiosis Programme's (NISP) Quick Wins workshops, which bring businesses together in a 'resource speed-dating' exercise. They enable networking between neighbors and reward attendance through business gain.

The Port of Barcelona's waste collection service is a good example of *wider co-operation*.[21] In place for many years, the service collects several waste streams from tenants. The waste collection service is yielding benefits including improved waste management compliance and reduced waste to landfill. Similarly, the Port of Felixstowe (fig. 3) has developed an innovative skip trailer which enables segregated waste to be collected from vessels at the quayside.[22] An email exchange with the port confirmed that the skip trailer has reduced collection costs and increased recycling rates.

*Longer-term capital infrastructure,* such as pipeline systems like the Botlek steam loop, require considerable investment and long term co-operative models to support a business case which may not yield immediate returns.

## Not just for big industrial areas

Research and practice also indicate that opportunities do exist to exploit resources across small-and medium-sized port areas and their vicinities. This might include provision of shared fa-

---

21 Jaume Gonzalez, 'Waste Management in the Port of Barcelona' (presentation at EcoPorts Foundation Conference, Genoa, December 2006).

22 G. Reeve, email exchange with author, 2009.

Fig. 4: The Bristol Port Estate area. *Source*: The Bristol Port Company

cilities, such as waste provision and exchange of resources between organizations.

What is key is taking the time to gain a working knowledge and understanding of the businesses and organizations within the area; sharing information about needs, requirements and residual resources; understanding the area's strengths, weaknesses, opportunities and threats and how these can be countered and built upon collaboratively.

Fowey Harbour Commissioners provide a good example.[23] Recognizing the negative impact of declining china clay exports, they have joined with local stakeholders to explore options for utilizing the significant volumes of china clay aggregate (a waste from quarrying) as a sustainable construction material.

### SevernNet

The research undertaken by Kate Royston led to a demonstration project across the Bristol Port estate area (fig. 4).[24] From an initial meeting in 2009 with five pilot businesses, the initiative

---

23  M. Sutherland, personal communication with author, 2009.
24  Royston, 'Application of Industrial Ecology across Port Areas'.

has grown and has engaged with more than 125 businesses and organizations across the area. Four of the pilot businesses (The Bristol Port Company, Siniat, ADM Milling and DS Smith Packaging) are core members of the Champions Steering Group.

Many of the businesses involved meet regularly and have benefitted from learning from and exchanging with each other. There is a feeling of increased empowerment, for example, to manage waste resources more effectively, and significant cost savings have been achieved. Toyota GB Portbury has transformed its waste practices and is close to zero waste to landfill. Business-to-business expertise is spreading in a number of areas — e.g. the deployment of LED lighting which can have a rapid payback — and there is a recognition that a lot more can be achieved.

The project is now established as a legal entity, SevernNet,[25] managed by a Champions Board. The agenda has been broadened to rebuild and strengthen links between the industrial and residential communities and to deal with their key challenges, such as getting more local people into local jobs, securing better employee travel facilities and supporting more sustainable development across the newly designated Avonmouth Severnside Enterprise Area.

## Self-interest to shared interest

The key to the success of SevernNet, and similar initiatives, is the recognition that more can be achieved from working together in a spirit of shared interest, rather than just self interest.

The re-establishment of links and co-operation between diverse communities of interest is vital in securing a resilient and effective local economy.

---

25 'SevernNet is a new enterprise bringing together businesses and community enterprises from Portbury, Avonmouth and Severnside': www.severnnet. org.

## In summary

Ports and their cities face increasing pressure to find new ways of managing the challenges of intensification, congestion and spiraling resource costs. This also presents a great opportunity to embrace alternative approaches. Industrial ecology is increasingly being demonstrated across the globe as a practical response, ideally suited to port city environments, leading to improved resource effectiveness, reductions in cost and environmental impact, and the emergence of 'greener' industry and economic diversification.

To take advantage of these opportunities requires new ways of thinking and acting for business, getting to know each other, building trust and working co-operatively and collaboratively. Getting started may not always be easy. It requires (a) champion(s), a facilitator and willingness for stakeholders to begin a process of positive engagement. Ideally, reaping the benefits also necessitates industrial ecology thinking to be embedded within strategic and spatial planning and new developments.

There is growing interest that the lessons being learnt could have wider application across Bristol and elsewhere, and opportunities for Plymouth should be explored as the new Plymouth Plan is developed!

Chapter 14

# Low-Carbon (Re-)Industrialization Lessons from China

*Kevin Lo and Mark Wang*

## Intoduction

The difference between (re-)industrialization in the past and present is that energy security and climate change now increasingly frame the space in which such processes take place. Therefore, there is an urgent need to rethink (re-)industrialization as part of a low-carbon future, rather than as something that perpetuates the current carbon-intensive mode of production and consumption. The aim of this chapter is to explore the concept of low-carbon industrialization, which has recently gained significant traction in China as part of the rethinking process. More specifically, this chapter seeks to clarify the meaning of low-carbon industrialization, supported by examples from China. The chapter also seeks to transfer lessons from China's experience with low-carbon industrialization to the context of (re-)industrialization. To anticipate the conclusion, this paper argues that both top-down and bottom-up initiatives can be important in low-carbon (re-)industrialization and that their appropriateness depends on the market structure and technological characteristics of the industry.

Following this short introduction, this chapter discusses energy security and climate change, which are the key challenges to (re-)industrialization. Next, it defines low-carbon industriali-

zation and illustrates the concept with the development of photovoltaic, wind turbine and solar water heater industries from
China. This chapter concludes with a discussion of the lessons
learnt from China's experience with low-carbon industrialization.

## Key challenges of re-industrialization: energy security and climate change

Improving energy security and tackling climate change are two
of the greatest challenges of the twenty-first century. One of the
key energy security concerns is peak oil, which refers to the
peaking or plateauing of the production of petroleum. Although
the timing of peak oil remains the subject of heated debate,
mainly due to uncertainty over the size of ultimate recoverable
reserves (especially in unconventional, but often controver-
sial places such as the Arctic), there is an increasing consensus
that high-quality, low-cost conventional oils are declining and
beginning to be substituted by low-quality, expensive sources
such as Alberta's tar sands and heavy oils in the Orinoco Delta.[1]
Coupled with the increasing demand from developing countries, oil prices are more than likely to continue to rise. Another
energy security concern is energy dependency upon politically
unstable territories.[2] Such concern has driven governments to
implement policies to reduce dependency on imported energy
by increasing the domestic supply of energy (which may or may
not be renewable) and reducing demand through energy conservation measures.

Climate change refers to significant and long-term changes
in the average weather patterns caused by the emission of greenhouse gases (e.g., carbon dioxide and methane), mainly from
the combustion of fossil fuels but also from non-combustion

---

1  Gavin Bridge. 'Geographies of Peak Oil: The Other Carbon Problem', *Geofo-rum* 41 (2010): 523–30.
2  Erica S. Downs. 'The Chinese Energy Security Debate', *China Quarterly* 177 (2004): 2–41.

sources such as non-energy industrial processes and agriculture, forest, and other land use (AFOLU). It is now generally accepted that the adverse effects of climate change include global warming, an increased likelihood and intensity of extreme weather events, and rising sea levels.[3] The internationally institutionalized climate change target, first established by the Copenhagen Accord (UNFCCC, 2009)[4] and subsequently ratified in the Cancun Agreements (UNFCCC, 2010),[5] is to constrain global temperature change to two degrees above the pre-industrial level. This temperature target could be achieved by a 450 ppm [parts per million] $CO_2$ stabilization level. The long lifetime of greenhouse gases, particularly $CO_2$, means that to achieve this target carbon emissions need to peak as soon as 2014.[6]

The two carbon problems are curiously contrasted, as noted by Bridge (2010), because energy security takes the form of flow constrictions and resource constraints, whereas climate change is fundamentally a problem of abundance and unrestrained flow. Nonetheless, energy security and climate change are connected by their relationships to the carbon-intensive mode of production and consumption. Prima facie, the two carbon problems appear to have made (re-)industrialization less desirable and viable as an urban development strategy due to the perceived energy intensity and carbon intensity of industrial activity. Using a general equilibrium model developed by the World Bank,

---

3   J. Houghton. *Global Warming: The Complete Briefing* (Cambridge: Cambridge University Press, 2004).

4   UNFCCC, Conference of the Parties (COP), *Report of the Conference of the Parties on its Fifteenth Session, Held in Copenhagen from 7 to 19 December 2009. Addendum. Part Two: Action Taken by the Conference of the Parties at its Fifteenth Session* (Geneva: United Nations Office, 2010), https://unfccc.int/documentation/documents/advanced_search/items/6911.php?priref=600005735.

5   UNFCCC, Conference of the Parties (COP), *Report of the Conference of the Parties on its Sixteenth Session, Held in Cancun from 29 November to 10 December 2010. Addendum Part Two: Action Taken by the Conference of the Parties at its Sixteenth Session* (Geneva: United Nations Office, 2010).

6   Chris Huntingford et al., 'The Link between a Global 2°C Warming Threshold and Emissions in Years 2020, 2050 and Beyond', *Environmental Research Letters* 7 (2012): 014039.

Mattot et al. (2011) estimated that even modest carbon control depresses industrial output by 3 to 3.5 percent and industrial exports by 5.5 to 7 percent for carbon-intensive countries such as China and India.[7] Arguments have been made that developing countries should bypass industrialization in pursuit of a service-oriented economy. However, it has also been argued that if the right path is taken, industrialization can contribute to the building of a prosperous, low-carbon future.[8] Zhang calls for a rethinking of industrialization as part of this future. As the world's largest carbon polluters, the concept of low-carbon industrialization is rapidly gaining currency in China as part of the rethinking process. This paper now turns to examine this concept.

## Low-carbon industrialization in China

There are in fact three meanings of low-carbon industrialization: (1) the decarbonization of existing carbon-intensive industries through energy conservation or carbon capture and sequestration; (2) the development of high-tech, high value-added and low-emission industries (e.g. biomedicine and information technology) and (3) the development of industries that manufacture low-carbon energy systems and infrastructures, such as products in energy efficiency (e.g. building insulation materials), renewable energy (photovoltaic and wind turbines) and climate adaptation. Because of the limitation of space, this chapter focuses on the third dimension of low-carbon industrialization, although it acknowledges that all three types are significant and useful responses to climate change. To further illustrate the level of complexity and variety even within this narrow definition of low-carbon industrialization, this chapter divides the abstract discussion into three examples: the photovoltaic industry, the

---

7   Aaditya Mattoo et al., 'Can Global De-Carbonization Inhibit Developing Country Industrialization?', *The World Bank Economic Review* 26 (2011): 296–319.

8   Zhang, L.-Y., 'Is Industrialization Still a Viable Development Strategy for Developing Countries under Climate Change?', *Climate Policy* 11 (2011): 1159–76.

wind turbine industry and the solar water heater industry. These examples are carefully chosen to demonstrate the diverse pathways through which low-carbon industrialization develops and evolves.

## The photovoltaic industry

Photovoltaic (PV) units convert sunlight into electricity by means of silicon-based materials. The PV production chain consists of upstream production (i.e. purification of silicon, casting silicon into ingots, and slicing ingots into wafers), which is capital- and technology-intensive and downstream production (i.e. assembling silicon wafers into cells and modules), which is energy- and labour-intensive.[9] Barriers to entry are high in upstream production but relatively low in downstream production, where entire turnkey production lines can be purchased and run without much prior experience. This provides a suitable entry point for Chinese start-ups such as Suntech, Yingli and Trina, which entered the downstream PV industry in the early 2000s. These private companies have been able to compete aggressively in the global market on a price basis, and have very quickly propelled China to be the world's largest PV cell and module manufacturer. However, China's position in upstream production remained weak until 2007, when China produced just 2.5 percent of the world's silicon.[10]Recently, Chinese firms have accumulated sufficient capital and technological know-how to venture upstream. By 2010, China had gained substantial market share in almost every step of the PV production chain: 33 percent of silicon processing, 52 percent of ingots and wafers, 50 percent of PV cells, and 28 percent of PV modules.[11] China's PV industry is export-oriented, with less than 10 percent of output

9   Arnaud De La Tour et al., 'Innovation and International Technology Transfer: The Case of the Chinese Photovoltaic Industry', *Energy Policy* 39 (2011): 761–70.
10  Ibid.
11  Alim Bayaliyev et al., *China's Solar Policy: Subsidies, Manufacturing Overcapacity & Opportunities* (Washington, DC: GW School of Public Policy and Public Administration, 2011), http://solar.gwu.edu/research/

absorbed domestically.[12] The export orientation of the PV industry reflects the lack of domestic installation — by the end of 2009, the cumulative installation of PV in China was 300 MW, equal to 3.3 percent of that in Germany.[13]

The development of the PV industry in China is largely a bottom-up affair. Until recently, Chinese authorities have done little to support the industry.[14] Rather, success is attributed to local entrepreneurialism, the recruitment of skilled executives from the Chinese diaspora, low energy and labour costs, and the subsidy of PV in Europe through generous feed-in tariffs.[15] The 2008 global financial crisis and the reduction in PV feed-in tariff and installation subsidies among European countries created problems with overcapacity and diminished profits. In response, the Chinese government introduced a series of supportive policies such as subsidized credit from state-owned banks.[16] Moreover, the government introduced direct subsidies and feed-in tariffs to boost domestic PV installation. Consequently, the cumulative PV installation in China skyrocketed from 300 MW at the end of 2009 to 3300 MW at the end of 2011, an increase by a factor of 11 over two years.[17] In 2012, the government promised to invest a further 15 billion RMB to increase PV installation by 5200 MW.[18] These policies have been instrumental in protecting the PV industry in China from collapse.

china%E2%80%99s-solar-policy-subsidies-manufacturing-overcapacity-opportunities

12 Bernardina Algieri et al., 'Going "Green": Trade Specialisation Dynamics in the Solar Photovoltaic Sector', *Energy Policy* 39: 7275–83.

13 Mo-Lin Huo and Dan-Wei Zhang, 'Lessons from Photovoltaic Policies in China for Future Development', *Energy Policy* 51 (2012): 38–45.

14 De la Tour et al., 'Innovation and International Technology Transfer'.

15 Ibid.; Bayaliyev et al., *China's Solar Policy*.

16 Jailu Liu and Don Goldstein, 'Understanding China's Renewable Energy Technology Exports', *Energy Policy* 52 (2013): 417–28.

17 Sufang Zhang and Yongxiu He, 'Analysis on the Development and Policy of Solar PV Power in China', *Renewable and Sustainable Energy Reviews* 21 (2013): 393–401.

18 Eric Savitz, 'China Solar Stocks Soar; Chinese Government Vows $2B in Subsidies', *Forbes*, December 12, 2012.

## The wind turbine industry

A wind turbine generation system (WTGS) generates electricity by capturing kinetic energy from wind to power a generator. Unlike the PV industry, the WTGS industry is vertically integrated and highly concentrated. In the early 2000s, four companies from Europe and the United States controlled the WTGS market: Vestas, Gamesa, Enercon and GE Wind.[19] Technical barriers to entry are high because the production of competitive WTGS requires specialized labour skills and technical know-how.[20] China forayed into the WTGS industry at approximately the same time as the PV industry, but through very different means. Foreign direct investment played a crucial role in the early days, with almost all leading companies investing in China.[21] Foreign WTGS makers were attracted to China because of the rapidly growing wind-power market driven by supportive policies, including direct subsidies and feed-in tariffs. Moreover, the requirement that at least 70 percent of the materials be sourced locally to be eligible for subsidies and feed-in tariffs practically forbade foreign companies from exporting components and turbines directly from China.[22] In short, the government created a condition that strongly incentivized foreign companies to establish production lines in China. In contrast to the PV industry, the WTGS industry in China is domestic-oriented, with very little export. The growth of the industry is thus inseparable from the strong, policy-driven growth in the domestic deployment of

---

19  Liu and Goldstein, 'Understanding China's Renewable Energy Technology Exports'.

20  Zhen-Yu Zhao, et al., 'Comparative Assessment of Performance of Foreign and Local Wind Turbine Manufacturers in China', *Renewable Energy* 39 (2012): 424–32.

21  Liu and Goldstein, 'Understanding China's Renewable Energy Technology Exports'.

22  Yuanchun Zhou et al., 'Joint R&D in Low-Carbon Technology Development in China: A Case Study of the Wind-turbine Manufacturing Industry', *Energy Policy* 46 (2012): 100–108.

WTGS, which became the world's largest in terms of cumulative capacity in 2010.[23]

Another interesting feature of the WTGS industry in China is the rapid rise of domestic manufacturers, which surpassed foreign-owned companies in China's WTGS market share in 2007 and secured a market share of 87 percent in 2010.[24] Joint research and development (R&D) projects are a key strategy of fast-track learning on the part of domestic manufacturers. Whereas the leading foreign companies invest directly in China to protect proprietary information, small-scale design and consulting firms usually collaborate with Chinese WTGS manufacturers in joint R&D. The acquisition of human capital is crucial to the process of technological transfer through joint R&D. For example, when the Shanghai Electric Company (SEC) and Aerodyn collaborated to design two MW wind turbines, SEC sent 30 engineers to Germany to receive professional training for one year.[25] Through the training, the engineers obtained a basic capacity to design wind turbines and gained knowledge about Aerodyn's technological foundation, such that they can collaborate with Aerodyn experts to design WTGSs that would satisfy local climatic requirements.

### Solar water heaters

Solar water heating (SWH) is a type of solar thermal technology used to heat water from direct sunlight. China's SWH industry has grown rapidly in the last decade. The annual SWH production increased from 6.1 million square meters in 2000 to 42 million square meters in 2009, making China by far the largest SWH manufacturer in the world.[26] A complete production chain has formed from raw material processing to final product assem-

---

23  Global Wind Energy Council, *Global Wind Report — Annual Market Update* (Brussels: Global Wind Energy Council, 2011), http://gwec.net/wp-content/uploads/2012/06/Annual_report_2011_lowres.pdf.

24  Zhou et al., 'Joint R&D in Low-Carbon Technology Development in China'.

25  Ibid.

26  Hu Runqing et al., 'An Overview of the Development of Solar Water Heater Industry in China', *Energy Policy* 51 (2012): 46–51.

bly. Vacuum-tube SWH, which relatively is less technologically intensive, dominates the market. Because the technological barriers are low, the industry is highly fragmented and competitive. There are over 5,000 SWH manufacturers in China, most of them limited in production capacity and product quality.[27] Nevertheless, a batch of large and influential enterprises has emerged in the sector, including four enterprises with an output value of 2 billion RMB.[28]

The most striking feature of the development of the SWH industry is that it is an entirely local initiative, with little reliance on the foreign market (unlike PV), foreign investments (unlike WTGS) and government intervention (also unlike WTGS). The key to success is that the SWH industry is able to produce products that can compete with traditional fuel-based water heaters on a price basis without the help of government subsidies. Using a life-cycle cost analysis of vacuum-tube SWH, Han et al. (2010) found that a household can save 342–3321 RMB in fuel costs annually, depending on household water use. Considering that SWHs are approximately 800–1,000 RMB more expensive than traditional water heaters, their payback period can be as brief as a few months. This economic competitiveness has led to a large domestic demand, with a 33 percent average annual growth rate of sales from 2006 to 2009.[29]

## Conclusions: lessons from China

The key lesson learnt from the present analysis of China's low-carbon industrialization is that there are many pathways of development. The PV industry was developed using the export-oriented model, primarily targeting the European market, which was booming thanks to generous feed-in tariffs. The development of the PV industry is mainly a bottom-up initiative,

---

27 Jingyi Han et al., 'Solar Water Heaters in China: A New Day Dawning', *Energy Policy* 38 (2010): 383–91.

28 Runqing et al., 'An Overview of the Development of Solar Water Heater Industry in China'.

29 Ibid.

with little involvement from the government until recently. The WTGS industry in China was developed with the help of direct foreign investment, either as wholly foreign-owned companies or as joint R&D projects. In either case, there has been a successful technology transfer to domestic companies, which now dominate the domestic market. The development of the WTGS industry is a top-down initiative, as government intervention is central, particularly in creating the conditions to attract foreign companies to China. The SWH industry was developed as a pure bottom-up initiative, with little involvement from foreign markets, foreign companies and government intervention. The success of the SWH industry lies primarily in its ability to outcompete traditional water heaters without the help of government subsidies.

To conclude, this chapter made two contributions to the discussion of (re-)industrialization in industrialized countries. First, it highlighted the imperative of rethinking (re-)industrialization in face of the two carbon problems; that of energy security and climate change. Second, this paper argued that low-carbon (re-)industrialization can be achieved through multiple alternative pathways. Both top-down and bottom-up initiatives can be important, and the appropriateness of the model depends on the market structure and technological characteristics of the industry.

# Bibliography

Additive Manufacturing Special Interest Group, *Shaping Our National Competency in Additive Manufacturing: A Technology Innovation Needs Analysis Conducted by the Additive Manufacturing Special Interest Group for the Technology Strategy Board*. London: Technology Strategy Board, 2012.

Artifex and Opifex. *The Causes of Decay in a British Industry.* London: Longmans, Green & Co., 1907.

Algieri, Bernardina, Antonio Aquino, and Marianna Succurro. 'Going "Green": Trade Specialisation Dynamics in the Solar Photovoltaic Sector'. *Energy Policy* 39, no. 11 (2011): 7275–283. doi:10.1016/j.enpol.2011.08.049.

Anderson, Chris. *Makers: The New Industrial Revolution.* New York: Crown Business, 2012.

Anonymous. 'Coming Home'. *The Economist,* January 19, 2013, http://www.economist.com/news/special-report/21569570-growing-number-american-companies-are-moving-their-manufacturing-back-united.

———. 'Press 1 for Modernity'. *The Economist.* April 28, 2012. http://www.economist.com/node/21553510.

Arieff, Allison. 'The Future of Manufacturing Is Local'. *The New York Times.* March 27, 2011. http://opinionator.blogs.nytimes.com/2011/03/27/the-future-of-manufacturing-is-local/.

Ashton, Thomas S. *An Eighteenth-Century Industrialist, Peter Stubs of Warrington: 1756–1806.* Manchester: Manchester University Press, 1939.

Badger, Emily. 'The Real Estate Deal That Could Change the Future of Everything'. *CityLab*. November 19, 2012. http://www.citylab.com/work/2012/11/real-estate-deal-could-change-future-everything/3897/.

Barndt, Karl. 'Memory Traces of an Abandoned Set of Futures: Industrial Ruins and the Post-Industrial Landscapes of Germany'. In *Ruins of Modernity*, eds. Julia Hell, Andreas Schönle, Julia Adams, and George Steinmetz, 270–93. Durham: Duke University Press, 2010.

Bayaliyev, Alim, Julia Kalloz, and Matt Robinson. *China's Solar Policy: Subsidies, Manufacturing Overcapacity & Opportunities*. Washington, DC: GW School of Public Policy and Public Administration, 2011. http://solar.gwu.edu/research/china%E2%80%99s-solar-policy-subsidies-manufacturing-overcapacity-opportunities

Bel, Germà. 'Against the Mainstream: Nazi Privatization in 1930s Germany'. *The Economic History Review* 1 (2010): 34–55.

Van Berkel, René. 'Regional Resource Synergies for Sustainable Development in Heavy Industrial Areas: An Overview of Opportunities and Experiences'. 2006. https://www.researchgate.net/publication/270340749_Regional_Resource_Synergies_for_Sustainable_Development_in_Heavy_Industrial_Areas_an_Overview_of_Opportunities_and_Experiences

Bluestone, Barry, and Bennett Harrison. *The Deindustrialization of America: Plant Closings, Community Abandonment, and the Dismantling Of Basic Industry.* New York: Basic Books, 1982.

Boltanski, Luc. *On Critique: Sociology of Emancipation.* Translated by G. Elliott. Cambridge: Polity Press, 2011

Boons, Frank. 'Self-Organization and Sustainability: The Emergence of a Regional Industrial Ecology'. *Emergence: Complexity and Organization* 10, no. 2 (2008): 40–47. https://journal.emergentpublications.com/article/self-organization-and-sustainability-the-emergence-of-a-regional-industrial-ecology/.

Boyer Brian, 'Pools are Expensive (Thoughts about the Long Tail and Crowdfunding)'. *Brickstarter,* March 26, 2012. http://brickstarter.org/pools-are-expensive-thoughts-about-the-long-tail-and-crowdfunding/.

———— and Dan Hill, *Brickstarter.* Helsinki: Sitra, 2013. http://www.brickstarter.org/Brickstarter.pdf.

Brenner, Neil, and Nik Theodore. 'Cities and the Geographies of "Actually Existing Neoliberalism."' In *Spaces of Neoliberalism: Urban Restructuring in North America and Western Europe,* eds. Neil Brenner and Nik Theodore, 2–32. Oxford: Blackwell Publishing, 2002.

Bridge, Gavin. 'Geographies of Peak Oil: The Other Carbon Problem'. *Geoforum* 41, no. 4 (2010): 523–30.

Bryson, John R. 'Obsolescence and the Process of Creative Reconstruction'. *Urban Studies* 34, no. 9 (1997): 1439–58.

————, P.W. Daniels, and B. Warf. *Service Worlds: People, Organisations, Technologies.* London: Routledge, 2004.

———— and Grete Rusten. *Design Economies and the Changing World Economy: Innovation, Production and Competitiveness.* London: Routledge, 2010.

———— and Michael Taylor. 'Mutual Dependency, Diversity and Alterity in Production: Cooperatives, Group Contracting and Factories'. *Interrogating Alterity: Alternative Economic and Political Spaces,* eds. D. Fuller, A.E. Jonas, and R. Lee, 75–94. Farnham: Ashgate, 2010.

Bunting, Madeleine. *Willing Slaves: How the Overwork Culture Is Ruling Our Lives.* London: HarperCollins, 2011.

Cameron, Jenny, and Julie Katherine Gibson-Graham. 'Feminising the Economy: Metaphors, Strategies, Politics'. *Gender, Place and Culture: A Journal of Feminist Geography* 10, no. 2 (2003): 145–57.

Capital Institute, *Field Guide to Investing in a Resilient Economy: Evergreen Cooperative Field Study.* 2012. http://fieldguide.capitalinstitute.org/uploads/1/3/9/6/13963161/_fs2-evergreen_8pg.pdf

Carey, Jeffrey. T*he Faber Book of Utopias,* ed. Jeffrey Carey, 276–78. London: Faber, 1999.

Carroll, Berenice A. *Design for Total War: Arms and Economics in the Third Reich.* The Hague: Mouton De Gruyter, 1968.

Chambers, J.D. *The Workshop of the World.* Oxford: Oxford University Press, 1961.

Chang, Ha-Joon. *Kicking Away the Ladder: Economic Development In Historical Perspective.* London: Anthem, 2002

Chomsky, Noam. *Occupy.* London: Penguin, 2012.

Christopherson, Susan. 'The Fortress City'. In *Post-Fordism: A Reader,* ed. Ash Amin, 409–25. Oxford: Blackwell, 1995.

City of Cleveland, *City of Cleveland 2012 Budget Book.* 2012. http://webapp.cleveland-oh.gov/aspnet/docs/get. aspx?id=988&file=2012Budget.pdf.

City of Cleveland, Department of Economic Development. *Report to Council 2010.* 2010. http://www.cdfa.net/cdfa/cd-faweb.nsf/ordredirect.html?open&id=clev2010report.html.

Clark, Jeniffer. *Working Regions: Reconnecting Innovation and Production in the Knowledge Economy.* London: Routledge. 2013.

Clarke, Jo, Mel Evans, Hayley Newman, Kevin Smith, and Glen Tarman (eds.). *Not If But When: Culture Beyond Oil.* London: Art Not Oil, Liberate Tate and Platform, 2011.

Cleveland Clinic. *Cleveland Clinic: A Vital Force in Ohio's Economy.* 2014. https://my.clevelandclinic.org/ccf/media/ Files/About-Cleveland-Clinic/economic-impact-report/ economic-impact-report-2015-Ohio.pdf?la=en.

Clift, Roland. 'Clean Technology and Industrial Ecology'. In *Pollution: Causes, Effects and Control,* ed. R.M. Harrison, 411–44. Cambridge: The Royal Society of Chemistry, 2001.

Clutter, McClain. 'Cleveland: Medi-Plex City'. In *Formerly Urban: Projecting Rust Belt Futures,* ed. J. Czerniak, 50–69 (New York: Princeton Architectural Press, 2013).

Court, W.H.B. *A Concise Economic History of Britain.* Cambridge: Cambridge University Press, 1965.

Crean, Sarah. 'In the Shadow of Real Estate, Linking Designers and Manufacturers in New York City'. *Progressive Planning* 190 (2012): 24–26.

Crooks, Ed. 'GE Takes $1bn Risk In Bringing Jobs Home'. *Financial Times*. https://www.ft.com/content/21a46546-78f1-11e1-88c5-00144feab49a.

Curtis, Fred. 'Eco-Localism and Sustainability'. *Ecological economics* 46, no. 1 (2003): 83–102.

Darley, Gillian. *Factory*. London: Reaktion Books, 2003.

Davis, Mike. 'US Elections — the New Deal?' *Socialist Review* 330 (2008): n.p., http://www.socialist review.org.uk/article.php?articlenumber=10589.

Deane, Phyllis M. *The First Industrial Revolution*. Cambridge: Cambridge University Press, 1979.

De La Tour, Arnaud, Matthieu Glachant, and Yann Ménière. 'Innovation and International Technology Transfer: The Case of the Chinese Photovoltaic Industry'. *Energy Policy* 39, no. 2 (2011): 761–70.

Demos, *People Make Place: Growing the Public Life of Cities*. London: Demos, 2005.

Dey, Roselin. 'Amsterdam: Sustainable City in the Making'. *Justmeans*. May 26, 2010. http://www.justmeans.com/blogs/amsterdam-sustainable-city-in-the-making.

Dicken, Peter. *Global Shift: Transforming the World Economy*. London: Sage, 2003.

Donald, James (ed.). *Imagining the Modern City*. London: Athlone, 1999.

Downs, Erica S. 'The Chinese Energy Security Debate'. *The China Quarterly* 177 (2004): 21–41.

Duranton, Gilles, and Diego Puga. 'Nursery Cities: Urban Diversity, Process Innovation, and the Life Cycle of Products'. *American Economic Review* (2001): 1454–77.

Easterling, Keller. 'Take-Away'. In *Perspecta 45: Agency*, eds. H. Evans, 157–60. Cambridge: MIT Press, 2012.

Edwards, Jason. 'The Materialism of Dialectical Materialism'. In *New Materialisms: Ontology, Agency and Politics*, eds. D. Coole and S. Frost, 281–97. Durham: Duke University Press, 2010.

Engelhardt, D. 'Sustainability in the Bio/Agro Industry: A Case Study'. In *Proceedings of the Institution of Civil Engi-*

neers-*Waste and Resource Management* 163, no. 1, (2010): 3–8. http://www.icevirtuallibrary.com/doi/pdf/10.1680/warm.2010.163.1.3.

Esping-Andersen, Gøsta. *Social Foundations of Postindustrial Economies.* Oxford: Oxford University Press. 2003.

European Commission. *Cities of Tomorrow: Challenges, Visions, Ways Forward.* Luxembourg: Publications Office of the European Union, 2011

———. *Committee on Spatial Development. European Spatial Development Perspective: Towards Balanced and Sustainable Development of the Territory of the European Union.* Luxembourg: Office for Official Publications of the European Communities, 1999.

———. *Creative Europe: The European Union Programme for the Cultural and Creative Sectors (2014–2020).* Brussels: Publications Office of the European Union, 2011.

———. *Crossing Borders — Connecting Cultures: The EU Culture Programme (2007–2013),* Brussels: Publictions Office of the European Union, 2011.

———. *Culture in Motion: The Culture Programme: 2007–2013.* Luxembourg: Communications Office of the European Union, 2010.

———. EUROPE *2020: A Strategy for Smart, Sustainable and Inclusive Growth.* Brussels: Publications Office of the European Union, 2010.

———. *European Agenda for Culture in a Globalizing World.* Brussels: Publications Office of the European Union, 2007.

———. *Inter-Service Group on Urban Development: The Urban Dimension in European Union Policies 2010, Introduction and Part 1: European Commission.* Brussels: Publications Office of the European Union, 2010.

———. *Promoting Sustainable Urban Development in Europe: Achievements and Opportunities.* Brussels: Publications Office of the European Union, 2009.

———. *State of the Innovation Union 2012: Accelerating Change.* Brussels: Publications Office of the European Unions, 2013.

————. *Towards an Urban Agenda in the European Union.* Brussels: Publications Office of the European Union, 1997.

————. *Unlocking the Potential of Cultural and Creative Industries.* Brussels: Publications Office of the European Union, 2010.

————. *Working Document: The European Agenda for Culture — Progress towards Shared Goals.* Brussels: Publications Office of the European Union, 2007.

European Union. *The Consolidated Treaties [and] Charter of Fundamental Rights.* Luxembourg: Publications Office of the European Union, 2010.

Evans, Chris. 'Merthryr Tyndif in the Eighteenth Century: Urban by Default'. In *Industry and Urbanization in Eighteenth-Century England,* eds. P. Clark, and P. Corfield, 11–18. Leicester: Leicester University Press, 1994.

Evans, Graeme. 'Creative Cities, Creative Spaces and Urban Policy'. *Urban Studies* 46, no. 5–6 (2009): 1003–40.

Faircloth, Kelly. 'At a Ribbon-Cutting for Shapeways' "Factory of the Future"'. Bloomberg Talks New York Tech'. *The Observer.* October 18, 2012. http://observer.com/2012/10/shapeways-grand-opening-factory-long-island-city-michael-bloomberg-mayor-3d-printing/

Florida, Richard. *Cities and the Creative Class.* New York: Routledge, 2005.

————. *The Rise of the Creative Class: And How It's Transforming Work, Leisure, Community and Everyday Life.* New York: Perseus Book Group, 2002.

———— and Irene Tinagli. *Europe in the Creative Age.* London: Demos, 2004.

Franzen, Carl 'NEA Weighs In On Kickstarter Funding Debate'. *Talking Points Memo.* February 27, 2012. http://talkingpointsmemo.com/idealab/nea-weighs-in-on-kickstarter-funding-debate.

Gershenfeld, Neil. 'How to Make Almost Anything: The Digital Fabrication Revolution'. *Foreign Affairs* 91, no. 6 (2012): 43–57.

Gibson-Graham, Julie Katherine *The End of Capitalism (As We Knew It): A Feminist Critique of Political Economy*. Minneapolis: University of Minnesota Press, 2006.

Global Wind Energy Council, *Global Wind Report — Annual Market Update*. Brussels: Global Wind Energy Council, 2011. http://gwec.net/wp-content/uploads/2012/06/Annual_report_2011_lowres.pdf.

Glyn, Andrew. *Capitalism Unleashed: Finance, Globalization, and Welfare*. Oxford: Oxford University Press, 2006.

Gonzalez, Jaume. 'Waste Management in the Port of Barcelona. Presentation at EcoPorts Foundation Conference in Genoa'. December 2006.

Gorz, André. *Farewell to the Working Class: An Essay on Post-Industrial Socialism*. Translated by M. Sonenscher. London: Pluto, 1982.

Gough, Jamie. 'Neoliberalism and Socialisation in the Contemporary City: Opposites, Complements And Instabilities'. *Antipode* 34, no. 3 (2002): 405–26.

Graeber, David. *Debt: The First 5,000 Years*. Brooklyn: Melville House, 2014.

Graham, Steven (ed.). *Disrupted Cities: When Infrastructure Fails*. London: Routledge, 2009.

——— and Simon Marvin. *Splintering Urbanism: Networked Infrastructures, Technological Mobilities and the Urban Condition*. London: Routledge, 2001.

Greater London Authority. *Supplementary Planning Guidance: Industrial Capacity*. London: Greater London Authority, 2008.

Hall, Paul. *Cities of Tomorrow: An Intellectual History of Urban Planning and Design in the Twentieth Century*. Oxford: Basil Blackwell, 1988.

Hall, Suzanne. *City, Street and Citizen: The Measure of the Ordinary*. London: Routledge, 2012.

Hamdi, Nabeel. *Small Change: About the Art of Practice and the Limits of Planning in Cities*. London: Earthscan, 2004.

Han, Jingyi, Arthur P.J. Mol, and Yonglong Lu. 'Solar Water Heaters in China: A New Day Dawning'. *Energy Policy* 38, no. 1 (2010): 383–91.

Haraway, Donna. 'Situated Knowledges: The Science Question in Feminism and the Privilege of Partial Perspective'. *Feminist Studies* 14 (1988): 575–99.

Hardt, Michael. 'The Common in Communism'. In *The Idea of Communism,* eds. Costas Douzinas and Slavoj Žižek, 131–44. London and New York: Verso, 2010.

———— and Antonio Negri. *Commonwealth.* Cambridge and London: The Belknap Press of Harvard University Press, 2009.

Harvey, David. *Rebel Cities: From the Right to the City to the Urban Revolution.* London and New York: Verso, 2012

————. *The Enigma of Capital and the Crises of Capitalism.* London: Profile, 2010

Hatherley, Owen. *A Guide to the New Ruins of Britain.* London: Verso. 2010

Heynen, Nikolas C., Maria Kaika, and Erik Swyngedouw. *In The Nature of Cities: Urban Political Ecology and the Politics of Urban Metabolism.* London: Routledge, 2006.

Hines, Colin. *Localization: A Manifesto.* London: Earthscan, 2000.

Holt, H. *The Art of Green Patchwork: European Ports Collaborate to Innovate Ports Adapting To Change (PATCH).* Green-Port: 2011. http://www.zeelandseaports.nl/nl/download/file:green-patchwork.htm.

Houghton, John. *Global Warming: The Complete Briefing.* Cambridge: Cambridge University Press, 1995.

Huntingford, Chris, Jason A. Lowe, Laila K. Gohar, Niel H.A. Bowerman, Myles R. Allen, Sarah C.B. Raper, and Stephen M. Smith. 'The Link Between a Global 2°C Warming Threshold and Emissions in Years 2020, 2050 and Beyond'. *Environmental Research Letters* 7, no. 1 (2012).

Huo, Mo-Lin, and Dan-Wei Zhang. 'Lessons from Photovoltaic Policies in China for Future Development'. *Energy Policy* 51 (2012): 38–45.

Jacobs, Jane. *The Death and Life of American Cities*. New York: Modern Library, 1961

―――. *The Economy of Cities*. London: Jonathon Cape. 1969

Jakob, Doreen. *Beyond Creative Production Networks: The Development of Intra-Metropolitan Creative Industries Clusters in Berlin and New York City*. Berlin: Rhombos, 2009.

―――. 'Constructing the Creative Neighborhood: Hopes and Limitations of Creative City Policies in Berlin'. *City, Culture and Society* 1, no. 4 (2010): 193–98.

―――. 'The Eventification of Place: Urban Development and Experience Consumption in Berlin and New York City'. *European Urban and Regional Studies* 20, no. 4 (2013): 447–59.

―――, '"To Have and To Need": Reorganizing Cultural Policy as Panacea for Berlin's Urban and Economic Woes'. In *The Politics of Urban Cultural Policy: Global Perspectives,* eds. C. Grodach and D. Silvereds, 110–21 (New York: Routledge, 2013).

Jarvis, Helen. 'Moving to London Time: Household Co-Ordination and the Infrastructure of Everyday Life'. *Time & Society* 14, no. 1 (2005): 133–54.

Jessop, Bob. "The Entrepreneurial City" in *Transforming Cities: Contested Governance and New Spatial Divisions,* eds. Nick Jewson and Susanne MacGregor, 28–41. London: Routledge, 1997.

Jünger, Ernst. *Der Arbeiter: Herrschaft und Gestalt*. Hamburg: Hanseatische Verlagsanstalt, 1941 [1932].

―――. *Robotnik: Panowanie i forma bytu*. Warsaw: PWN, 2010.

―――. 'Total Mobilisation'. In *Krieg und Krieger*. Berlin: Junker und Dunnhaupt, 1930.

Kaika, Maria. *City of Flows: Modernity, Nature and the City*. New York: Routledge. 2005,

Kunicki, Wojciech. *Rewolucja konserwatywna w Niemczech 1918–1933*. Poznań: Wydawnictwo Poznańskie, 1999.

Kumar, Krishan. *From Post-Industrial to Post-Modern Society: New Theories of the Contemporary World*. Second Edition. Malden: Blackwell Publishing, 2005.

Kumar, Sanjay, and J.P. Kruth. 'Composites by Rapid Prototyping Technology'. *Materials & Design* 31, no. 2 (2010): 850–56.

Landry, Charles. *The Creative City: A Toolkit for Urban Innovators.* London: Comedia, 2008.

———— and Franco Bianchini. *The Creative City.* London: Demos, 1995.

Lammers, J. *Seaports as Turntables towards Sustainability: Policy Letter on Sustainable Seaports.* Directoraat-Generaal Luchtvaart en Maritieme Zaken, Ministerie van Verkeer en Waterstaat, 2008.

Lange, Alexandra. 'Against Kickstarter Urbanism'. *The Design Observer.* May 2, 2012.

Lee-Smith, Diana. 'Cities Feeding People: An Update on Urban Agriculture in Equatorial Africa'. *Environment and Urbanization* 22, no. 2 (2010): 483–99.

Lefebvre, Henri. *Critique of Everyday Life.* Vol. 3. Translated by G. Elliott. London: Verso, 2008.

————. *Dialectical Materialism.* Translated by J. Sturrock. Minneapolis, London: University of Minnesota Press, 2009.

————. 'Right to the City'. In *Writings on Cities,* trans. E. Kofman and E. Lebas, 147–59. Oxford: Blackwell, 2000.

————. *The Production of Space.* Translated by D. Nicholson Smith. Oxford: Blackwell, 2010.

————. *The Urban Revolution.* Minneapolis: University of Minnesota Press, 2013.

Legg. S. (ed.). *Spatiality, Sovereignty and Carl Schmitt: Geography of the Nomos.* London: Routledge, 2011.

Leslie, Esther. 'Tate Modern: A Year of Sweet Success'. *Radical Philosophy* 109 (2001): 2–5.

Lipietz, Alain. 'Fears and Hopes: The Crisis of the Liberal-Productivist Model and Its Green Alternative'. *Capital & Class* 37, no. 1 (2013): 127–41.

Liu, Jialu, and Don Goldstein. 'Understanding China's Renewable Energy Technology Exports'. *Energy Policy* 52 (2013): 417–28.

Lorentzen, Anne. 'Cities in the Experience Economy'. *European Planning Studies* 17, no. 6 (2009): 829–45.

Marcuse, Paul. 'What Has to Be Done? The Potentials and Failures of Planning: History, Theory, and Actuality. Lessons from New York'. *AnArchitektur* 14 (March 2005): 36–40.

Marsh, Peter. 'Hopes for Growth in Manufacturing', *The Financial Times,* May 29, 2011. https://www.ft.com/content/9627941a-8a13-11e0-beff-00144feab49a.

Massey, Doreen. *World City.* Cambridge: Polity Press, 2007

Mattoo, Aaditya, Arvind Subramanian, Dominique van der Mensbrugghe, and Jianwu He. 'Can Global De-Carbonization Inhibit Developing Country Industrialization?' *The World Bank Economic Review* 26 (2011): 296–319.

McDowell, Linda, Diane Perrons, Colette Fagan, Kath Ray, and Kevin Ward. 'The Contradictions and Intersections of Class and Gender in a Global City: Placing Working Women's Lives on the Research Agenda'. *Environment and Planning* A 37, no. 3 (2005): 441–61.

Miles, Steven. *Spaces for Consumption: Pleasure and Placelessness in the Post-Industrial City.* London: Sage, 2010.

Mistry, Nisha. *Newark's Manufacturing Competitiveness.* Washington, DC: Brookings Institute, 2013. https://www.brookings.edu/wp-content/uploads/2016/06/NewarkManufacturingMay28.pdf.

Moss, Ian. 'Art and Democracy: The NEA, Kickstarter, And Creativity In America'. *Createquity.* April 9, 2012. http://createquity.com/2012/04/art-and-democracy-the-nea-kickstarter-and-creativity-in-america.html.

Myers, Garth. *African Cities: Alternative Visions of Urban Theory and Practice.* London: Zed Books. 2011.

OCAP, CO₂ *voor de tuinbouw — Factsheet 2012.* 2012. http://www.ocap.nl/files/Ocap_Factsheet2012_UK.pdf.

Owen, David, J.D. Chambers, and William Ashworth. *The Workshop of the World: British Economic History from 1820 to 1880.* London: Oxford University Press, 1961.

Peck, Don. 'Can The Middle Class Be Saved?' *The Atlantic.* September 2011. https://www.theatlantic.com/magazine/archive/2011/09/can-the-middle-class-be-saved/308600/?single_page=true.

Peck, Jamie, and Adam Tickell. 'Neoliberalizing Space'. *Antipode* 34, no. 3 (2002): 380–404.

Philadelphia Industrial Development Corporation, *An Industrial Market and Land Use Strategy for the City of Philadelphia — Executive Summary.* 2010. http://www.phila.gov/commerce/Documents/Philadelphia%20Industrial%20Land%20and%20Market%20Strategy.pdf

Pieterse, Edgar. *City Futures: Confronting the Crisis of Urban Development.* London: Zed Books, 2008.

Pittsburgh City Council, *City of Pittsburgh Pennsylvania Budget 2011.* 2011. http://www.city.pittsburgh.pa.us/main/assets/budget/2011/2011-Operating-Capital-Budget.pdf.

Pine, B. Joseph, II. *Mass Customization: The New Frontier in Business Competition.* Boston: Harvard Business Press, 1993.

Port of Rotterdam. 'Innovative Use of Space Looking for Environmental Advantages'. 2016. https://www.maasvlakte2.com/en/index/show/id/696/sustainable-layout.

———.'Port Wants Steam Pipe For $CO_2$ Reduction'. November 22, 2009. http://www.portofrotterdam.com/en/News/press-releases-news/Pages/20091126_01.aspx.

Prest, John M. *The Industrial Revolution in Coventry.* London: Oxford University Press, 1960.

Prigann, Herman. 'Prologue — Thoughts about Nature'. In *Ecological Aesthetics: Art in Environmental Design: Theory and Practice,* eds. Heike Strewlow, Hermann Prigann, Vera David, 79–90. Basel: Birkhäuser, 2004.

Rakowski, Tomasz. *Łowcy, zbieracze, praktycy niemocy: Etnografia człowieka zdegradowanego* [Hunters, Gatherers, Practicioners of Feebleness: An Etnography of Degraded Man]. Gdańsk: Słowo/Obraz Terytoria, 2009.

Ratner, S. 'An Inquiry into the Nazi War Economy, Review of Design for *Total War: Arms and Economics in The Third Reich,* by Bernice A. Carroll' *Comparative Studies in Society and History* 12, no. 14 (1970), 466–72.

Rifkin, Jeremy. 'The Third Industrial Revolution: How the Internet, Green Electricity, and 3-D Printing Are Ushering In a Sustainable Era of Distributed Capitalism'. *World Financial Review* 1 (2012): 4052–57.

————. *The Third Industrial Revolution: How Lateral Power Is Transforming Energy, the Economy, and the World*. New York: Palgrave Macmillan, 2011

Robinson, Jennifer. *Ordinary Cities: Between Modernity and Development*. Oxford: Routledge, 2006.

Rotterdam Climate Initiative, *Full Steam Ahead! Rotterdam Climate Initiative: 2008 Report — Summary*. Rotterdam: Rotterdam Climate Initiative, 2009. http://www.rotterdam-climateinitiative.nl/documents/ samenvatting%20Op%20 Stoom%20EN.pdf

Rowlands, Marie B. *Masters and Men: In the West Midland Metalware Trades before the Industrial Revolution*. Manchester: Manchester University Press, 1975.

Royston, Kate. *Application of Industrial Ecology across Port Areas: The Potential to Leverage Commercial Advantage and Support Sustainable Development in sw England*. MSc Thesis, University of Surrey, 2011.

Runqing, Hu, Sun Peijun, and Wang Zhongying. 'An Overview of the Development of Solar Water Heater Industry in China'. *Energy Policy* 51 (2012): 46–51.

Sassen, Saskia. *Cities in a World Economy*. Third Edition. Thousand Oaks: Pine Forge Press, 2006.

Savitz, Eric. 'China Solar Stocks Soar; Chinese Government Vows $2B in Subsidies'. *Forbes*. December 12, 2012.

Scott, Allen, and Michael Storper. 'Regions, Globalization, Development'. *Regional Studies* 37, no. 6–7 (2003): 579–93.

Seabright, Paul. *The Company of Strangers: A Natural History of Economic Life*. Princeton: Princeton University Press, 2004.

Sennett, Richard. *The Corrosion of Character: The Personal Consequences of Work in the New Capitalism*. New York and London: W.W. Norton. 1998.

————. *The Craftsman*. New Haven: Yale University Press, 2008.

Sharzer, Greg. 'Local Resistance to Global Austerity: It Will Never Work'. *openDemocracy*, January 3, 2013. http://www.

opendemocracy.net/ourkingdom/greg-sharzer/local-resist-
ance-to-global-austerity-it-will-never-work.

———. *No Local: Why Small-Scale Alternatives Won't Change
the World*. Winchester: Zero Books, 2012.

Sicakkan, H.G. *Diversity and the European Public Sphere—Towards a Citizens' Europe*. EUROSPHERE Final Comparative Study, Vol. 3 (2013). http://www.eurosphere.uib.no/
files/2010/07/EUROSPHERE_Final-Report_Web_version2.
pdf.

*SkyMall*, Late Spring Catalogue (Phoenix: SkyMall, 2013)

Smit, Jac, and Joe Nasr. 'Urban Agriculture for Sustainable
Cities: Using Wastes and Idle Land and Water Bodies as
Resources'. *Environment and Urbanization* 4, no. 2 (1992):
141–52.

Smith, Stephen A. *The Russian Revolution: A Very Short Introduction*. Oxford: Oxford University Press, 2002.

Sweezy, Marine. *The Structure of the Nazi Economy*. Cambridge: Harvard University Press, 1941.

Swyngedouw, Erik. *Designing the Post-Political City and the
Insurgent Polis*. London: Bedford Press, 2011.

Tausch, Arno. *Titanic 2010: The European Union and Its Failed
Lisbon Strategy* (Hauppauge: Nova Science Publishers,
2010).

*Time* staff, 'Jack Ma'. *Time*. February 28, 2000. http://content.
time.com/time/world/article/0,8599,2054856,00.html.

UNFCCC, Conference of the Parties (COP), *Report of the Conference of the Parties on its Fifteenth Session, Held in Copenhagen from 7 to 19 December 2009. Addendum. Part Two:
Action Taken by the Conference of the Parties at its Fifteenth
Session*. Geneva: United Nations Office, 2010. https://
unfccc.int/documentation/documents/advanced_search/
items/6911.php?priref=600005735.

———. *Report of the Conference of the Parties on its Sixteenth
Session, Held in Cancun from 29 November to 10 December
2010. Addendum Part Two: Action Taken by the Conference
of the Parties at its Sixteenth Session*. Geneva: United Nations Office, 2010.

Urhahn Urban Design, *Industry in the City: A Report for the London Development Agency and Greater London Authority*. Amsterdam: Urhahn Urban Design, 2010.

Vihvelin, Kadri. 'Arguments for Incompatibilism'. *Stanford Encyclopedia of Philosophy*. Spring 2011 Edition. Edited by Edward N. Zalta. http://plato.stanford.edu/entries/incompatibilism-arguments/.

Walker, Rob. 'The Trivialities and Transcendence of Kickstarter'. *New York Times*. August 7, 2011. http://www.nytimes.com/2011/08/07/magazine/the-trivialities-and-transcendence-of-kickstarter.html.

Wallerstein, Immanuel. *World-Systems Analysis: An Introduction*. Durham: Duke University Press, 2006.

Wohlers, Terry T. *Rapid Prototyping & Tooling: State of the Industry: Annual Worldwide Progress Report*. Fort Collins: Wohlers Associates, 2001.

Woodward, Christopher. *In Ruins*. London: Vintage, 2002.

Yan, Xue, and P. Gu. 'A Review of Rapid Prototyping Technologies and Systems'. *Computer-Aided Design* 28, no. 4 (1996): 307–18.

Zardini, Mirko (ed.). *Sense of the City: An Alternate Approach to Urbanism*. Baden: Lars Müller Publishers, 2005.

Zhang, Le-Yin. 'Is Industrialization Still a Viable Development Strategy for Developing Countries under Climate Change?' *Climate Policy* 11, no. 4 (2011): 1159–76.

Zhang, Li. *Strangers in the City: Reconfigurations of Space, Power, and Social Networks within China's Floating Population*. Stanford: Stanford University Press, 2001.

Zhang, Sufang, and Yongxiu He. 'Analysis on the Development and Policy of Solar PV Power in China'. *Renewable and Sustainable Energy Reviews* 21 (2013): 393–401.

Zhao, Zhen-Yu, Wen-Jun Ling, George Zillante, and Jian Zuo. 'Comparative Assessment of Performance of Foreign and Local Wind Turbine Manufacturers in China'. *Renewable Energy* 39, no. 1 (2012): 424–32.

Zhou, Yuanchun, Bing Zhang, Ji Zou, Jun Bi, and Ke Wang. 'Joint R&D in Low-Carbon Technology Development in

China: A Case Study of the Wind-Turbine Manufacturing Industry". *Energy Policy* 46 (2012): 100–108.

Zukin, Sharon. *Loft Living: Culture and Capital in Urban Change.* Baltimore: John Hopkins University Press, 1982.

———. *Naked City: The Death and Life of Authentic Urban Places.* Oxford: Oxford University Press, 2010.

# About the Contributors

## Editor

**Krzysztof Nawratek** is a senior lecturer in Architecture at the School of Architecture, the University of Sheffield, United Kingdom. Educated as an architect and urban planner, he has worked as a visiting professor at the Geography Department at the University of Latvia and as a researcher at National Institute for Regional and Spatial Analysis, Maynooth, Ireland. He was a member of the Board of Experts European Prize for Urban Public Space 2012, 2014 and 2016 and a member of the selection panel for the Polish contribution to the 13th International Architecture Biennial in Venice in 2012 and to the 14th in 2014. Krzysztof Nawratek is an urban theorist, author of *City as a Political Idea* (Plymouth, University of Plymouth Press, 2011), *Holes in the Whole: Introduction to the Urban Revolutions* (Winchester, Zero Books, 2012) and Radical Inclusivity. Architecture and Urbanism (ed. Barcelona, dpr-barcelona, 2015) several papers and chapters in edited books.

## Contributors

**Karl Baker** is a consultant in urban and transport planning at MRCagney, Auckland, New Zealand. He has previously contributed to architectural and planning strategies that incorporate industrial workspace in mixed-use developments in London. His research on urban reindustrialization was initially undertaken as part of his MSc City Design and Social Science completed at the London School of Economics and Political Science in 2011. He has held positions at the Future Cities Catapult, London, LSE Cites and the New Zealand Ministry of Transport. His current work and research interests focus on the political economy of urban planning policy and economic evaluation of transport infrastructure.

**John R. Bryson** is Professor of Enterprise and Competitiveness and Director of the City-Region Economic Development Institute, Birmingham Business School, University of Birmingham, UK. He research initially focused on the rise and role of business and professional services (BPS), but since 2005 has explored the changing economic geography of manufacturing in developed market economies. This research has explored the interactions between BPS and manufacturing and, in particular, the role design plays in the competitiveness of manufacturing firms. His books include Service Worlds: People, Organisations, Technologies (Routledge); Hybrid Manufacturing Systems and Hybrid Products (IMA/ZLW & IfU); Design Economies and the Changing World Economy (Routledge) and Industrial Design, Competition and Globalization (Palgrave).

**Jennifer Clark** is an Associate Professor in the School of Public Policy and the Director of the Center for Urban Innovation at the Georgia Institute of Technology. Her research focuses on regional economic development, manufacturing, industrial districts and innovation. Her first book, *Remaking Regional Economies: Power, Labor, and Firm Strategies in the Knowledge Economy* (with Susan Christopherson) won the Best Book Award from the Regional Studies Association in 2009. Her newest book, *Working Regions: Reconnecting Innovation and Production in the Knowledge Economy* (2013) focuses on policy models aimed at rebuilding the links between innovation and manufacturing in the US

**Michael Edwards** is an economist and planner at the Bartlett School, UCL. He works with the Just Space network of activist groups on London Planning and the London economy (http://justspace.org.uk) and blogs at http://michaeledwards.org.ukwhere his publications are also listed. Active on Twitter @ michaellondonsf

**Alison Hulme** is an associate researcher at the Centre for the Study of the Moral Foundations of Economy and Society at University College Cork, Ireland. She has previously held posts at Royal Holloway, UK; University of Otago, New Zealand; University College Dublin, Ireland. She is the author of *On the Commodity Trail* (Bloomsbury Academic, 2015) and various journal articles. Prior to entering academia, Alison was a radio and TV presenter for many years.

**Doreen Jakob** is an artist and scholar at UNC Chapel Hill, USA and at the University of Exeter, UK. She has held research positions at the Centre for an Urban Future in New York City, at the Urban Research Program at Griffith University, Brisbane, Australia, at the Centre for Metropolitan Studies in Berlin, for the German Research Foundation, for the Emmy Noether Program and, most recently, with the UK Arts and Humanities Research Council. Doreen received her PhD from Humboldt University Berlin.

**Jeffrey T. Kruth** is an urbanist and educator based at Kent State University's Cleveland Urban Design Collaborative (CUDC) where he contributes to the research, design, and teaching aspects of the practice. Prior to joining the CUDC he practiced in New Haven, CT, building affordable housing, and worked at the Yale Urban Design Workshop. His work explores the intersections of cultural landscapes, economics, politics, & technology.

**Karol Kurnicki** is an post-doctoral researcher at the Institute of Sociology, Jagiellonian University, Poland. He currently researches socio-spatial processes of bordering and differentiation in large urban housing estates. He was a visiting researcher at the Culture Theory Space Research Cluster, University of

Plymouth (2012) and The Centre for Urban Conflicts Research, University of Cambridge (2014). He is one of the founders of Zakład Usług Miejskich (Urban Workshop) association. Main academic interests include urban studies, urban sociology and critical sociology.

Kevin Lo is an Assistant Professor at the Department of Geography, Hong Kong Baptist University. As a human geographer with a research focus on environmental governance and politics, Kevin is interested in the relationship between authoritarianism and environmentalism, and the development of effective policy interventions and governance mechanisms to promote renewable energy and energy efficiency. He has published in many leading journals, including *Renewable and Sustainable Energy Reviews, Energy Policy, Energy for Sustainable Development, Energies, Environmental Science & Policy, Habitat International,* and *Cities.*

Malcolm Miles is author of *Limits to Culture* (2015), *Eco-Aesthetics: Art, Literature and Architecture in a Period Of Climate Change* (2014), and *Herbert Marcuse: An Aesthetics of Liberation* (London, Pluto Press, 2011). His next book is *Cities & Literature* (2017/18); he is researching a future book on radical aesthetics from Romanticism to contemporary critical art practices, and maintains an interest in modernist painting and architecture.

Rachel Mulhall is Research Fellow at the Business School, University of Birmingham, UK. Her research interests focus on the firm, competitiveness and the regional economy. Current work is focused on understanding the spatial and contractual structure of supply chains, business adjustment and risk management.

Christina Norton a founder and director of Fluid, whose creative practice has contributed to new attitudes towards architecture, planning and creative practice. The work is founded on live research and user participation and ranges from large-scale regeneration, neighbourhood planning and urban strategies to hybrid programmes and interventions to one off architectural projects. In 2007 Christina with fellow director Steve McAdam established Soundings to offer stand alone public consultation, acting as an impartial voice in the development process. In 2011 Fluid conceived and delivered Industri[us] an interim use strategy for vacant sites to revalue waste materials, bring back the economic, social and civic and help communities back on their feet. Between 1985–2009 Christina taught at the Architectural Association and London Metropolitan University, she was a founder of NATØ the 1980's avant-guard architecture group.

**Kate Royston** is an independent researcher, facilitator and advisor now based in south-western England. During 2006/7 she worked with the EcoPorts Foundation in Amsterdam which sparked a lasting interest in port areas and finding sustainable solutions to their environmental challenges. This ongoing research was partly undertaken as her dissertation project in part fulfilment of the MSc in Sustainable Development (University of Surrey) completed in 2011.

**Tatjana Schneider** is a researcher, writer and educator based at the School of Architecture in Sheffield, UK. She is co-founder of the research centre 'Agency' and was founder member of the workers cooperative G.L.A.S. (Glasgow Letters on Architecture and Space), which aimed to construct both a theoretical and practical critique of the capitalist production and use of the built environment. Her current work focuses on the changing role of architects and architecture in contemporary society, (architectural) pedagogy and spatial agency. She has an interest in theoretical, methodological and practical approaches that expand the scope of contemporary architectural debates and discourses by integrating political and economic frameworks that question normative ways of thinking, producing and consuming space. She is the (co)author of *Spatial Agency. Other Ways of Doing Architecture* (2011), *Flexible Housing* (2007), *A Right to Build*

(2011), (co)editor of *Agency. Working with Uncertain Architectures* (2009) and *glaspaper* (2001–2007).

**Myfanwy Taylor** is writing her PhD on contested urban economies at University College London. Her thesis argues that the rise of concern about affordable workspace in London is creating common ground for new economic alliances to emerge. It highlights the importance of the economic evidence base underpinning city strategies and plans as a key site of contestation, in which emerging economic alliances draw on their own perspectives and experiences to advance their interests and concerns. Myfanwy pursues a collaborative approach to research and has been working with a range of community planning networks in London including Just Space and groups in Tottenham and Newham. She is a member of the International Network of Urban Research and Action (INURA) and the Participatory Geographies Research Group of the RGS-IBG.

**Jonathan Vickery** is Associate Professor in the Centre for Cultural Policy Studies, at the University of Warwick, UK. With a background in contemporary art and design, he has taught and published on art and architectural history and theory, design, urbanism and organization studies. He was a co-editor of the journal Aesthesis, is now Chair of the international Art of Management and Organization conferences. He was co-director of the Shanghai City Lab (2013–2015), and is now a founder director of the new urban culture initiative Kalejdoskop East-West. At Warwick he is Director of the masters in Arts, Enterprise and Development. His most recent book (co-edited with Ian King) is *Experiencing Organisations* (Libri: Oxon).

**Mark Yaolin Wang** is a Professor in the School of Geography at the University of Melbourne. He is the author of *Mega Urban Regions in China* (1998) and the co-author of *China's Transition to a Global Economy* (2002), *China's Urban Space* (2007), *Old Industrial Cities Seeking New Road of Reindustrialisation* (2013), *Transforming Chinese Cities* (2014), and *Towards Low Carbon*

*Cities in China* (2014). He is also credited with numerous articles in the fields of geography, migration and urban studies.

www.ingramcontent.com/pod-product-compliance
Lightning Source LLC
Chambersburg PA
CBHW050652270326
41927CB00012B/2985